A PRAYER BOC

A PRAYER BOOK OF DAYS

Gregory K. Cameron

CANTERBURY
PRESS
Norwich

First published in 2024 by the Canterbury Press Norwich
Editorial office
3rd Floor, Invicta House
110 Golden Lane
London EC1Y 0TG, UK

www.canterburypress.co.uk

Canterbury Press is an imprint of Hymns Ancient & Modern Ltd
(a registered charity)

Hymns Ancient & Modern® is a registered trademark of
Hymns Ancient & Modern Ltd
13A Hellesdon Park Road, Norwich,
Norfolk NR6 5DR, UK

Scripture quotations are from The ESV Bible (The Holy Bible, English
Standard Version), copyright © 2001 by Crossway, a publishing ministry
of Good News Publishers. Used by permission. All rights reserved.

British Library Cataloguing in Publication data
A catalogue record for this book is available
from the British Library

ISBN 978-1-78622-595-5

CONTENTS

For my father, Kenneth Hughes Cameron,
who supported and encouraged me,
and enabled me to become who I am today.

INTRODUCTION

Christians are called to pray. Not only does the witness of the Old Testament speak of the joy that flows out of faithful prayer, but both Jesus and the authors of the New Testament spoke of the power of prayer. In the Old Testament, Psalm 34 begins with the words: 'I will bless the LORD at all times; his praise shall continually be in my mouth', while in the New Testament Paul the Apostle urges us to 'pray without ceasing' (1 Thessalonians 5.17). Jesus himself commended prayer to his followers, and promised that prayer would be effective (Matthew 21.22).

Prayer is nothing more and nothing less than resting in the presence of God, an intentional focus of our minds upon our creator and redeemer, and the offering up to him of the cry of our hearts. It is the intimate cry of the child to their parent. Jesus compared praying to the request of a child:

> Ask, and it will be given to you; seek, and you will find; knock, and it will be opened to you. For everyone who asks receives, and the one who seeks finds, and to the one who knocks it will be opened. Or which one of you, if his son asks him for bread, will give him a stone? Or if he asks for a fish, will give him a serpent? If you then, who are evil, know how to give good gifts to your

> children, how much more will your Father who is in heaven give good things to those who ask him! (Matthew 7.7 – 11)

Nevertheless, many Christians find it difficult to find the words to use in prayer. The disciples themselves acknowledged the problem (Luke 11.1), and Jesus taught them a simple prayer which quickly passed into widespread use in the earliest Christian communities (see Chapter 2).

Down through the centuries, Christian disciples have often found themselves drawing on the prayers of others to assist them in drawing close before the throne of God. This volume offers a month's supply of some of the most cherished prayers of the Christian family. Each chapter provides an adaptation that I have made of these prayers and, as in previous books, each chapter is headed with an icon or illustration of a figure, if not the actual author about whom I write, then of a saint or holy figure most associated with the prayer, or its traditional context. Scripture and prayer often intertwine, and where that happens, I hope to point it out, but above all else the purpose of this volume is to give us a resource of prayers, and to tell the stories that lie behind them.

As we work through the book, we also work through the Christian centuries, beginning with the tradition of prayer into which Jesus was born, and arriving at last in our own century. All prayer is offered in a context, and sometimes it helps us to know how a prayer came into being.

As I compiled these prayers, I became acutely aware of the fact that if I were to include some of our best-known prayers, then there was a preponderance of authors who were from Europe and the Middle East, and male. I have tried to include significant examples of prayers written by women, but I hope to compile another volume in the future which could redress this balance, and draw on the global diversity of Christian prayer. For now, I hope this selection will suffice, and share with you a small part of the enormous depth of heritage of prayer that has been passed down to us to aid us in our own faltering approach to the throne of God's grace.

+Gregory Llanelwy
Easter 2024

ONE

DAVID
The Book of Psalms

I start with a prayer that is older than Christianity, possibly by as much as a thousand years. It is attributed in the Bible to King David, who may have lived in the tenth century BC. This prayer is included in the Book of Psalms in the Old Testament, and it is included here because the psalms are the prayers that Jesus prayed, and were often used by him. The Book of Psalms has been called 'The Hymn Book of the Second Temple', the Temple of Solomon as rebuilt by the Jewish people after their return from exile in Babylon. The Book of Psalms is a collection of one hundred and fifty songs and prayers that has been known, loved, memorised and used daily by Jews and Christians for over two thousand years. For us to recite the psalms, therefore, is to join ourselves to every generation of Christians who has gone before us, and to the Jewish tradition of prayer, and the prayers of every synagogue service.

Jesus will have grown up hearing the psalms recited in the synagogue, and probably at home by his family. He used them himself, and we know that Jesus knew the particular psalm I have chosen for this chapter (Psalm 35), because he is described as quoting from it in the Gospel according to John (John 15.25).

The psalms have always been popular as prayers because they are texts that Christians believe have been inspired by the Holy Spirit; they are God-breathed. However, they are also popular because of their realism. They don't varnish the emotions experienced by human beings, and themselves express sadness, anger, fear, doubt, competition and disappointment. All these are offered to God with a raw honesty. It is only when we offer God the depth of who we are, and the reality of our feelings, that we are truly open to his grace.

Psalm 35 is a psalm of opposition, and like many of the psalms it speaks from a place where the author feels the pain of persecution. Like many Hebrew prayers, and many of the psalms, its verses are expressed in parallels – ideas are expressed twice in succession, in slightly varying language and vocabulary. (To emphasise this parallelism, I have placed parts of the text of the psalm below in italics, where the ideas repeat in this pattern.)

It is dangerous to guess at what went on within Jesus' mind, but we do know that he recognised that his ministry faced severe opposition, and that in trying to be faithful to God, he was going to face those who sought to attack him, and even silence him.

Reading the psalm ourselves, we may feel that it doesn't sound very holy to call down God's vengeance on our enemies, but that is the point: the psalm speaks from the place of anger and fear where better emotions about our enemies are not in the forefront of our mind. God takes us as we are. Prayer is not about posing for God, but accepting that all thoughts are known to him. Being honest in our prayers opens us to God's transforming grace.

This prayer is honest therefore about the difficulties that the psalmist faces, but equally expresses total confidence in the power of God to transform the situation. The psalm eagerly waits for the action of God, expectant of his help and his grace.

For us, there are a number of lessons here. We are called, first of all, to be honest in our prayers to God, and not to mask the depth of our feelings. However, we too must learn to trust in God, and be expectant to see his help and grace at work in our lives. We must invite God to help us transcend the paucity of our strength with the knowledge that God is our security and our strength. Finally, in praying the psalms, we are joining our prayers to those of Jesus. We stand in his place before God, and join him in prayers that were familiar to him, who intercedes for us before the throne of God. As he prayed, so we pray also.

Although I have chosen one psalm to include among this collection, I can recommend the regular recitation of the psalms, and their study, to all those who wish to develop ways of praying. They give us a vocabulary that will sustain us in our own prayers, and they can lead us through the themes of praise and worship, of lament and disappointment, of resilience in the face of opposition, and the delights of finding a home amongst God's people.

The icon I have included in this chapter is of King David, adapted from a picture by the seventeenth-century Spanish artist Pedro de Berruguete. David is an intriguing character – at once both ideal king of Israel and flawed leader. His adultery with

Bathsheba and his betrayal of her husband, Uriah the Hittite, as well as his attitude to power, show him to be unscrupulous at times, and yet he always came back to obedience to God, and seeking his blessing. We don't really know his connection to the Book of Psalms, but at least seventy-three psalms are ascribed to his authorship.

David is like so many of us, a mixture of pride, ambition, faith, doubt and the desire to know God better, so that he is a fit companion and prayer partner.

As we say Psalm 35, let us be honest about where we experience fear or opposition, whether in our daily life or in the internal spiritual battles against our worst impulses. We can place ourselves into the hands of God, our maker and our redeemer, seeking a deeper faith and trust in his promise to assist us in life.

Contend, O Lord, with those who contend with me;
fight against those who fight against me!
Take hold of shield and buckler and rise for my help!
Draw the spear and javelin against my pursuers!
Say to my soul, 'I am your salvation!'
Then my soul will rejoice in the Lord,
exulting in his salvation.
All my bones shall say, 'O Lord, who is like you,
delivering the poor from him who is too strong for him,
the poor and needy from him who robs him?'
How long, O Lord, will you look on?
Rescue me from their destruction,
my precious life from the lions!
I will thank you in the great congregation;
in the mighty throng I will praise you.

Let not those rejoice over me who are wrongfully my foes,
and let not those wink the eye who hate me without cause.
You have seen, O LORD; be not silent!
O LORD, be not far from me!
Awake and rouse yourself for my vindication,
for my cause, O my God and my Lord!
Let those who delight in my righteousness
shout for joy and be glad
and say evermore, 'Great is the LORD,
who delights in the welfare of his servant!'
Then my tongue shall tell of your righteousness
and of your praise all the day long.

(*Psalm 35, selected verses*)

TWO

JESUS
The Lord's Prayer

Father,
May your name be revered,
and your sovereignty be established.
As your will is done in heaven,
so let it be done on earth.
Give us bread for living,
enough to see out the day.
Forgive us our sins,
in the manner that we forgive those in debt to us.
Do not lead us into testing,
but deliver us from the wicked.

(Adapted from Luke 11.2–4)

The Lord's Prayer is by far and away the single most well-known Christian prayer of all time. This is hardly surprising, as Jesus offers the prayer as an explicit answer to the request of his followers to teach them to pray (Luke 11.1–4). Its simplicity offers an easy model to follow. This single prayer unites Christians across the globe and down through the centuries. Its frequent use makes it a pebble so well-worn and smooth that we can recite it without thinking about the words, and we usually repeat them in the form that we were taught in childhood.

The translation we most commonly use in English closely follows the translation from the Latin Vulgate version of the Bible provided by John Wycliffe in 1389 as part of his project to provide the whole New Testament in the language people could understand. A new translation therefore can shock us when we see afresh the prayer's directness. At the beginning of this chapter I've put a translation that I've attempted in my own words. I hope that it reminds us about the power and simplicity of the prayer, which can be lost beneath the varnish of frequent use.

In the Lord's Prayer we see how Jesus drew on the pattern of the psalms by using parallelism, and the synagogue tradition of the invocation of God's protection in daily life. Jesus himself seems to have had an aversion to over-complicated prayers (Matthew 6.7), although he spent many hours at the start of the day in prayer (Mark 1.35). It appears that in all things he wished to align himself to God's will (John 5.19), and this theme features strongly in the prayer, while taking an intimate approach to God, greeting him as Father.

The prayer begins by focusing on God in worship, literally offering worth-ship, acknowledging the greatness of God, and moves on to a straightforward dependency on God for sufficient food, forgiveness and protection. It fits in precisely with

Jesus' other teaching – about the priority that must be given to God's kingdom in the lives of his followers (Matthew 6.33), and reliance on the fact that God will provide (Matthew 6.8).

The Lord's Prayer appears in two versions in the Gospels – a shorter form in the Gospel according to Luke, and a longer version in the Gospel according to Matthew, with the addition of two further lines. Interestingly, Catholic Christians have become more used to the Lukan version, while Protestants tend to use the Matthean version. Matthew includes a 'doxology', an ascription of authority to God, returning to the opening theme to close the prayer. There is a third ancient version, which appears in a book called the *Didache* (see Chapter 4), and which is so close to the passages from the Gospels that it demonstrates how widely the Lord's Prayer was learned and repeated even within the first hundred years of Christianity:

> Our Father in heaven, sanctified be your name, let your kingdom come, as your will is done in heaven, so on earth; for our bread, give us sufficient for today, write off our debts as we write off those in debt to us, lead us not into trials, yet rescue us from that which is evil, for yours are the power and the glory for all ages. (Didache 8.2)

To accompany this chapter, I offer an icon of Christ. In the church of the first millennium, there was a lot of discussion about the appropriateness of images of Jesus, which were at times regarded as an offence against the second commandment (Exodus 20.4–6) In the end, the churches came to believe that the incarnation of Jesus, the Word of God being born and living as a human being, was best expressed and defended by allowing images of Jesus to be created. Originally a clean-shaven youth in appearance, after a century or two the image of Jesus changed radically to that of bearded and mature man, perhaps influenced by relics such as the Turin Shroud. Such an image is probably more faithful to Jesus' Jewish origins and the fashions of Jewish men in the first century. Many people, in praying, find it helpful to hold in mind the image of the Son of Man and Son of God, he who was born, lived and died for our sake.

As we say the Lord's Prayer, we can remember that we are joining Jesus and his disciples in a prayer that belonged to them, and with the same simplicity of faith, which entrusts all thing into God's hands, and seeks to make the coming of his kingship a priority in our lives.

Our Father, who art in heaven,
Hallowed by thy name,
Thy kingdom come,
Thy will be done,
On earth as it is in heaven.
Give us this day our daily bread.
And forgive us our trespasses,
As we forgive those who trespass against us.
And lead us not into temptation,
But deliver us from evil.
For thine is the kingdom, the power and the glory,
For ever and ever. Amen.

(Matthew 6.9–13, traditional version)

THREE

MARY
Magnificat

The Bible contains many prayers in addition to the Book of Psalms. One such prayer, the prayer of Mary, appears in the Gospel according to Luke. This has also entered the bloodstream of Christian worship and is known as the Magnificat. This prayer takes its name from its first word in Latin, meaning 'it magnifies', or 'it enlarges', in the sense that Mary offers up the entirety of her soul in the praise of God.

The Magnificat also demonstrates again for us how much Christian prayer derives from the Hebrew tradition. There are clear parallels drawn between the story of the young virgin chosen to be the Mother of God, and her response of praise when she shares the news of her pregnancy (Luke 1.39–56), and the story of Hannah in the Old Testament, and her hymn of praise to God on discovering that she is pregnant with a chosen servant of God (1 Samuel 2.1–11). Not only do strong similarities appear between the Song of Hannah and the Song of Mary in their construction and the ideas they express, but they also set an example of how God is praised in the Bible, recounting his actions in history to bring salvation to his people.

What is particularly striking is that salvation is seen in very human terms in these songs – God intervenes in human history to assert the work of his saving power amongst the weakest and poorest in society. We sometimes hear complaints when Christian leaders comment on the evils of society and advocate social justice, and yet both the Jewish and Christian scriptures are remarkable for their interest in justice in this world, and what has been called 'God's preference for the poor'. Certainly, as the apostolic writer James puts it in his letter, included in the New Testament: 'If anyone says, "I love God", and hates his brother, he is a liar; for he who does not love his brother whom he has seen cannot love God whom he has not seen. And this commandment we have from him: whoever loves God must also love his brother' (1 John 4.20–21).

As Christian prayer evolved, and established patterns settled down for the recitation of scriptural prayers, the Magnificat found its home in the service of Vespers, or Evening Prayer, where it took its place as a 'canticle', a scriptural song that forms the core of daily prayers in the Church.

The icon I have illustrated for this chapter is one of the best known. Mary, the Mother of God, cradles her child, Jesus, and they interact as mother and child, each beloved to the other. This intimate relationship is at the heart of Christianity. Mary, who physically gave birth to the incarnate Lord of all, has a unique relationship with Jesus, but it nevertheless mirrors the intimate connection that God desires for all of us, and indeed for all of creation. It is, and it is intended to be, revolutionary.

As we pray the Magnificat, let us seek to enlarge the place of God's Spirit in our lives, and commit ourselves to be part of God's overturning of human order in his kingdom, to see justice done, and those who are poorest find their rightful place at the feast of God's kingdom.

My soul magnifies the Lord,
    and my spirit rejoices in God my Saviour,
for he has looked on the humble estate of his servant.
    For behold, from now on all generations will call me blessed;
for he who is mighty has done great things for me,
    and holy is his name.
And his mercy is for those who fear him
    from generation to generation.
He has shown strength with his arm;
    he has scattered the proud in the thoughts of their hearts;
he has brought down the mighty from their thrones
    and exalted those of humble estate;
he has filled the hungry with good things,
    and the rich he has sent away empty.
He has helped his servant Israel,
    in remembrance of his mercy,
as he spoke to our fathers,
    to Abraham and to his offspring for ever.

(*Luke 1.46–55*)

FOUR

THE *DIDACHE*
A Eucharistic Prayer

A number of documents have survived to the present day which date from the period immediately after the lifetime of the Apostles, and which bear witness to the life of the early Christian churches and the way in which the earliest Christians prayed. One of these documents is known as the *Didache* – in translation 'The Teaching (of the Twelve Apostles)'. It is an odd collection of instructions, advice and prayers for the life of the churches. Most scholars date it to the late first century, or the very early second century – around the time that the last books of the New Testament were being completed, preserved and collected together.

The *Didache* offers fascinating insights into the life and problems of the early Church – its problems in particular, because it is always the problems that attract the most comment! The book therefore emphasises what were regarded as the most important matters in the life of the Church, and gives us a snapshot of how the Church was run. It is evident that the Eucharist was a central part of the earliest Christians' life of worship, and the *Didache* contains some of the earliest prayers of consecration for the bread and wine of the Eucharistic feast about which we know.

This chapter is headed by an icon of one of the earliest saints of the period just after the apostles, St Polycarp. We do not know whether there is any connection between Polycarp and the *Didache*, but he lived at exactly the right time to be a contemporary of the text. St Irenaeus, one of the great writers of the late second century of the Christian era, recounts the story of Polycarp, and tells us that he had listened to the teaching of the Apostle John. A letter by Polycarp survives, the Letter to the Philippians (not the same as the one in the New Testament), which was discovered bound together with an account of how Polycarp was martyred for his faith when he was eighty-six years old. The church of the *Didache*, and the prayers written in it, belong therefore to his time, and take us back to a world where the first generation of Christian disciples, who had followed Jesus during his life, were handing on the faith to those who believed without having seen Jesus himself (John 20.29).

I have selected a text from the *Didache* which is one of the very earliest of the prayers of consecration of the elements of bread and wine which are used at the Eucharist.

In inviting you to pray these prayers, there is a reminder that when we use them, we join into a tradition that goes back to Jesus himself, and two thousand years of the liturgy of the Church. Their repetitive nature could seem heavy-handed compared with a modern text, but there is a deep sense of honouring and worshipping God in these prayers. Down through the centuries, Christians are defined by many things, but particularly by what they do in worship – taking bread and wine as Jesus did at the Last Supper, giving thanks, and obeying his command to 'Do this in remembrance of me.'

In taking this cup, we give you thanks, our heavenly Father, for the Vine of your servant David, which is made known to us through Jesus your Son. To you be glory even unto the end of the ages.

In taking this bread, we give thanks to you, our Father, for the life and knowledge that has been made known to us through Jesus your Son. To you be glory even unto the end of the ages. Just as the grain for this bread was once broken and scattered upon the mountains, and was gathered together to become one loaf, so gather your people together in your Kingdom from the ends of the earth, for to you belongs the glory and the power through Jesus Christ even unto the end of the ages.

O Master all powerful, dwelling outside of all creation, by your power food and drink is given for the enjoyment of humanity so that we might live thankfully unto you. Grant us also the spiritual food and drink and the gift of eternal life through Jesus your Son.

We give thanks to you because you are all powerful and to you belong glory now and even unto the end of the ages. Holy Father, your name now dwells in the hearts of your people and with it the knowledge and faith of eternal life which is revealed to us through Jesus your Son. To you be glory even unto the end of the ages.

Remember, O Lord, your gathered people. Rescue them from all evil and perfect them in your love. Gather your people from the four winds, and make us worthy of the kingdom that you have prepared, because yours is the power and the glory even unto the end of the ages. May your grace be upon us, and let this world pass away. Hosanna to the God of David. Let all those who are holy come now before the Lord, or else, let them repent. Come, Lord. Amen.

(*Adapted from the* Didache*, Chapters 9 and 10*)

FIVE

THE LITURGY OF ST MARK
Prayers for God's People

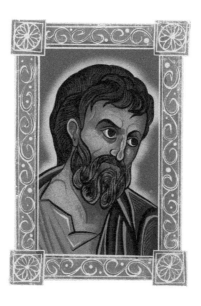

As we have already seen in the last chapter, the early Church placed great importance on the authenticity of its witness to what had happened in the life, death and resurrection of Jesus Christ. Passing on the memoirs of the Apostles became the core of tradition, a term that literally means the 'handing on' of a precious treasure.

A great deal of energy was given in the early centuries to being faithful to the apostles, and what was understood as 'the deposit of faith' (cf. Jude 3). It led to the compilation, for example, of the Apostles' Creed, probably at Rome, which purported to be a summary of the Apostles' teaching, so much so that in later centuries each phrase was said to have been contributed by one of the apostles in turn themselves.

However, there were many writings that looked like scripture circulating in the early Church, and one way to invest them with authority and legitimacy was to claim a link with the apostles. In the end, the Church only authenticated four of the many lives of Jesus that were circulated. The Gospels of Matthew, Mark, Luke and John were recognised as being distinctively authoritative and reliable. The evangelists Matthew and John were understood to be the actual disciples of Jesus, and Luke was recognised as a companion of St Paul. Mark is believed to have been John Mark, mentioned amongst the followers of the apostles. He was believed to have become a disciple of St Peter, eventually collecting and writing down Peter's memoirs of Jesus. Such a description goes back to the beginnings of Christianity in the writing of Papias (in the first century) and Irenaeus (in the second). In the same way, the various churches sought to attest to their founding by the apostles or their followers, so that the Church of Rome was said to have been founded by St Peter.

In Egypt, the Church of Alexandria traced its foundations to St Mark, and some of the most ancient prayers and liturgies of that Church are described as 'The Liturgy of St Mark', although they can only be traced back to documents of the fourth century. They may already have been preserved by generations of use, however. In later years, the See of Alexandria evolved into the Coptic Church, which flourishes in Egypt and elsewhere to this day, and it still preserves and uses this liturgy, one of the most ancient to survive.

In the icon of Mark at the head of this chapter, based upon the traditional pattern, we see the passion and dedication of a young man who is an inheritor of the witness of the apostles, and who has known the work of Christ in his own life.

I have chosen two prayers from the Liturgy of St Mark for our attention in this chapter. They speak of some of the central concerns of the early Church: fidelity to the apostles' teaching, the unity of all those called to follow Jesus, and prayer for the coming of God's kingdom. These early prayers of the Church are remarkable for the way in which they are faithful to the words of scripture, even when the earliest manuscripts of the scriptures themselves actually date from later in the life of the Church. In the short prayers offered in this chapter, there are references to texts in the Gospels according to Matthew and to John, the letters of Paul, and the Letter to the Hebrews.

As we pray these prayers, we can unite ourselves to these first Christians, and endeavour to share their enthusiasm to serve God by following Jesus, and obeying his teaching in our lives.

O Sovereign and Almighty Lord, bless all your people, and all those who are your flock. Pour out your peace, your help, and your love unto us your servants, the sheep of your fold, that we may be united in the bond of peace and love, one body and one spirit, in one hope of our calling. We ask this in your divine and boundless love.

O Sovereign Lord Christ Jesus, the co-eternal Word of the eternal Father, who was made in all things like as we are, but without sin, for the salvation of our race; you who have sent forth your holy disciples and apostles to proclaim and teach the gospel of your kingdom, and to heal all disease, all sickness among Your people: be pleased now, O Lord, to send forth your light and your truth. Enlighten the eyes of our minds, that we may understand your divine oracles. Fit us to become hearers, and not only hearers, but doers of your word, that we, becoming fruitful, and yielding good fruit from thirty to a hundred fold, may be deemed worthy of the kingdom of heaven.

(*Adapted from the Liturgy of St Mark*)

SIX

JOHN CHRYSOSTOM
A Prayer Before Reading the Bible

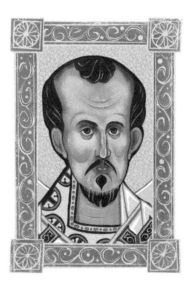

In the fourth century, Christianity had been transformed by the conversion of the Emperor Constantine, who was the first Roman Emperor to confess his Christian faith in public. Bishops became power brokers in the life of empire, which was a very mixed blessing, as with power came the temptation to corruption, and the office of bishop became a focus of worldly ambition.

Nonetheless, there remained some incredible figures of faith such as John, who was made Archbishop of Constantinople in AD 397. John had gained a reputation as an eloquent preacher during his years of ministry in Antioch, one of the great cities of the eastern Mediterranean. In his preaching, he emphasised a straightforward interpretation of scripture, and applied the principles of faith to practical issues in life. For this, he was awarded a very special nickname – Chrysostom, the Golden Mouthed. The icon with which I have headed this chapter shows the traditional representation of John, one that is immediately recognisable, with his large domed forehead and goatee beard.

By the standards of today, John's style can seem heavy and convoluted, and it is not easy read his words with the passion and intensity with which they may have been preached from the pulpit. It is said that John could hold large congregations entranced by his command of oratory and of the application of scripture.

Like many of those acknowledged as saints by the Church, John was far from perfect, conditioned by the morals of his times – he held views that are shocking when it came to the treatment of Jewish minorities, for example. However, he was popular with the crowds for standing up for the poor against the rich, and for making practical ways of living out Christian faith clear to those who listened to him.

In our own day, the word 'religion' is often given a bad name, in contrast to 'spirituality'. Religion correctly understood, however, isn't about the institutional versus the personal, but about how we apply our faith to life. As the Apostle James wrote in the biblical book named after him: 'Religion that is pure and undefiled before God and the Father is this: to visit orphans and widows in their affliction, and to keep oneself unstained from the world' (James 1.27). Religion therefore is the way in which we take our faith and apply it to life, and it was this at which John was so very good. It was John who also warned about the need to root our Christian faith in the realities of life: 'If you cannot find Christ in the beggar at the church door, you will not find him in the chalice.' He had a healthy scepticism of Church authority: 'The road to Hell is paved with the bones of priests and monks, and the skulls of bishops are the lamp posts that light the path.'

We can learn from John what it is to speak the truth to power, and to give unflinching witness to the truth of the gospel. His outspoken denunciation of the luxuries indulged in by members of the imperial court earned him the wrath of the Empress Eudoxia. Famously, when she made her anger known, John instead of backing down, spoke even more vehemently about the issue and her denunciation of him, comparing her to the corrupt queen Herodias. The tale is told in the Gospels about the betrayal and execution of St John the Baptist (Mark 6.17–27), and John Chrysostom in his sermon skilfully inserts himself as a John-the-Baptist-like figure: 'Again Herodias raves, again she demands the head of John the Baptist on a platter' he is said to have declaimed.

In the end, the Emperor became convinced that John was too much of a thorn in his side, and he was banished from Constantinople to a remote part of Asia Minor. His fearless defence of Christian faith however was treasured, and about 700 sermons and 240 letters by John survive to this day. Today, John is recognised as one of the three holy fathers of Eastern Christianity, the greatest teachers of Orthodox faith from the early centuries of the Church's life, ranked alongside Basil the Great and Gregory Nazianzen.

I have chosen a very simple prayer by John for us – a prayer to be used as we approach the reading of the Bible. As we pray this prayer, we can ask God to help us to understand the Bible with the clarity he gave to John the Golden Mouthed, and the ability to see how God wants us to amend our lives and discipleship to follow him more closely.

On you I set my hope, O my God, asking that you will enlighten my mind and my ability to understand with the light of your knowledge, so that I may not only cherish those things that are written, but do them, for you are the enlightenment of all those who lie in darkness, and from you in the end comes every good deed and every gift. Amen.

SEVEN

AUGUSTINE OF HIPPO
'Lord, Make Me Good, But Not Yet.'

To complement the three Holy Fathers of the East, Western Christianity recognised four Doctors (or Teachers) of the Church based in the Western tradition, Saints Ambrose, Augustine, Gregory the Great and Jerome. Of these, the most influential in the development of theology was Augustine, the great teacher and theologian who was a bishop in north Africa.

Augustine was of north African descent, and was born to a Christian mother, Monica, and to a Roman father, who converted to Christianity only on his deathbed. We know a great deal about Augustine's life, because of the major work of autobiography that he composed called *The Confessions*, in which he offers to God an account of his life, and how eventually he submitted to God's will. Augustine had a brilliant intellect, and was educated in the best schools of Carthage. It was in this period that he explored questions of philosophy and theology, although his first conversion was to the religion called Manichaeism. A man of ambition, he first travelled to Rome to seek to establish a fee-paying school there, but he was called to become a Professor of Rhetoric in Milan, then the capital of Italy, as the Emperors based themselves nearer to the borders of an Empire under threat from barbarians.

In Milan Augustine came into contact with the brilliant bishop and teacher, Ambrose, who won him for Christianity. At this moment in his journey of faith, Augustine realised that to follow Jesus meant that he had to bring his life into line with the moral teachings of scripture, despite the fact that he had a long-term partner, with whom he had had a son, Adeodatus. It was in this period that he uttered his most famous prayer, sometimes quoted as 'Lord, make me good, but not yet.' He had begun to recognise that his commitment to Christ required a holy life, but found it hard to abandon those elements of his life which kept him comfortable, even if they were contrary to his calling. It was a dilemma that makes Augustine so very real and human to us today, and with which many disciples of Jesus can identify.

In AD 387 Augustine finally committed himself to Christianity and, having been baptised by Ambrose, returned to north Africa, to preach and teach there. Quickly becoming famous for his preaching, Augustine was called to become Bishop of the city of Hippo in north Africa. He demonstrated admirable commitment to his new calling, selling off most of his inherited riches, and establishing a monastic community in his family home.

Augustine lived at a critical moment for the Roman Empire, and he watched as the Roman Province of North Africa was invaded by barbarian tribes, and later he died during one of the prolonged sieges of his city. During this period he completed another great work, *The City of God*, which described how, amidst earthly turmoil, and the downfall of worldly power, God's foundation of the heavenly city, and the life of the people of God, could not be overcome. In his writings and preaching, Augustine became the pre-eminent interpreter of the Christian faith for the western Roman Empire, and set in place many of the foundational building blocks of Christian theology which are still current.

We cannot be sure what Augustine looked like. The picture at the head of this chapter draws on one of the iconographic traditions for Augustine, which emphasises his long life of faith, and sees him carrying the wisdom of an older man. In common with many of the philosophers of his day, Augustine is shown with a beard, symbolic of his commitment to learning, and despising fashionable and expensive daily shaves.

Augustine's life and teachings are inspirational and still foundational for many Christians. One prayer attributed to Augustine has become hugely popular down through the centuries, because it speaks of our dependence upon God, and the joy we may find in him, while describing faith as a journey, which takes us from knowing God, to loving him, and through loving him to serving him. It articulates the paradox at the heart of Christian discipleship, that the more obedient we become to God's will for our lives, actually the more free we become, for Christian life is not unlike the skill of a talented musician: the more they give themselves to the discipline of learning and practice, the greater their ability to use their instrument to play music in any style or mood. As Jesus himself said: 'whoever does not take his cross and follow me is not worthy of me.

Whoever finds his life will lose it, and whoever loses his life for my sake will find it (Matthew 10.38–39). So it is that when we become truly obedient to God, we discover that we can become most fully and most freely the person we hope to be, and the person God calls us to be.

Everlasting Lord,
you are the light of the minds that know you,
the joy of the hearts that love you,
and the strength of the souls that serve you;
help us so to know you that we may truly love you,
and so to love you that we may fully serve you,
whose service is perfect freedom,
through Jesus Christ our Lord. Amen.

EIGHT

PATRICK

St Patrick's Breastplate

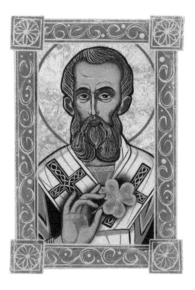

By the fifth century, the Christian faith was reaching the far edges of the Roman world. History indicates that Christianity reached the Roman province of Britannia fairly early on, and there is evidence of Christian art and architecture in the Province of Britannia, such as the mosaic of Christ found in Hinton St Mary, in Dorset, which is dated to the fourth century. However, in the fifth century a young Roman citizen of Britannia was captured by pirates, and trafficked as a slave to Ireland. Having served in slavery as a farmhand for a number of years, the young man managed to escape, and while travelling on the continent of Europe, entered a Christian monastic community, and became ordained. His sense of call drew him back to Ireland, where he spent the rest of his life preaching the Christian faith. Like Augustine, he wrote his confessions, and we know a great deal about his mission. His name was Patrick, and in later centuries he became recognised as the patron saint of Ireland.

It was not easy to establish the Christian faith in Ireland, and Patrick became famous for his exploits defending the Christian faith, attacking local paganism, and surviving many attempts on his life. The icon of Patrick at the head of this chapter depicts the mature saint, holding a shamrock, a plant intimately connected with Patrick after he had supposedly used its threefold leaf as a demonstration of the Christian doctrine of the Trinity, through which Christians understand God as both three and one.

Patrick is seen today as the exemplar of a specific style of Christian faith, known as Celtic spirituality because it is believed to have flourished across the three Celtic nations of the Isles of Britain. It is difficult to know how far what is described as Celtic spirituality is a modern reading into the past, since it is seen as being in harmony with contemporary themes of the wholeness of creation and environmental concerns, but there does seem to be a strong theme in the prayers that have survived which express a strong connection between the reve-lation of God in Christ and the revelation of God in creation.

However, Celtic spirituality was also strongly ascetic – there was a heavy emphasis on the struggle to be holy, and on punishing the body with austerity, a trait that sits less comfortably with modern manners. There was a profound sense of Christian faith as a battle against the spiritual powers of evil and tempta-tion, which drew on Paul's teaching about the Christian soldier putting on the whole armour of God (Ephesians 6.11–18). A number of prayers took the form of a 'lorica', which literally means body armour, but which is a prayer invoking God's protection. It is part of the conviction of Celtic faith that the powers of God could be relied upon to defend the Christian in their earthly journey, and one such lorica, written in the Irish of the eighth century, became particularly linked with Patrick, and specifically with the occasion when he invoked the protection of God against his opponent, Lóegaire, the king of Tara. It is known today as 'St Patrick's Breastplate' and is typical of Celtic faith in expressing its Trinitarian foundation.

The lorica, or breastplate, of St Patrick, begins with a strongly Trinitarian invocation, which was clearly a central part of Patrick's faith. It is a lengthy prayer, of which I quote only a part, but there is so much of depth in it that it seems sad to curtail it too much, as Patrick, or its true author, invokes so much of the revelation of God, in scripture and creation, to come to his defence. It is a reminder that we can be secure in our belief that God is on the side of all those who call upon him, that even the hairs of our head are numbered and precious in his sight (Luke 12.7). It is a reminder to see Christ in all whom we encounter (Matthew 25.31–40).

I rise today in the mighty strength of the invocation of the Trinity,
Through faith in the Three in One,
and confession of the One in Three,
Creator of creation.

I rise today
Through the strength of Christ's birth and baptism,
Through the strength of His crucifixion and His burial,
Through the strength of His resurrection and His ascension,
Through the strength of His descent
for the judgement of doom.

I rise today
Through the strength of the love of the seraphim,
of the obedience of angels, and the service of archangels,
In the prayers of the patriarchs,
and the predictions of the prophets,
In the preaching of apostles, and the faith of confessors,
In the innocence of holy virgins, and the deeds of righteous folk.

I rise today supported by the strength of heaven,
The light of the sun, and the radiance of the moon,
The splendour of fire, and the speed of lightning,
The swiftness of wind, and the depth of the sea,
The stability of the earth, and the firmness of rock.

I rise today, through
God's strength to pilot me, and God's might to uphold me,
God's wisdom to guide me, and God's eye to look before me,
God's ear to hear me, and God's word to speak for me,
God's hand to guard me, and God's shield to protect me,
God's host to save me from the snares of the devil,
From the temptation of vices, and from all who may wish me ill.

Christ go with me,
Christ before me, Christ behind me,
Christ within me, Christ beneath me,
Christ above me,
Christ on my right hand, Christ on my left hand,
Christ when I lie down, Christ when I rise,
Christ in the heart of every man who thinks of me,
Christ in the mouth of everyone who speaks of me,
Christ in every eye that sees me,
Christ in every ear that hears me.

NINE

JOHN CLIMACUS
The Jesus Prayer

As Christianity grew in power and worldliness following the conversion of the Roman Emperors and their patronage of Christian leaders and buildings, a counter-balancing movement away from the world developed in which individual Christians withdrew into deserted places. Those who sought out the desert in Egypt and the Middle East, or even the deserted places of a sparsely populated Europe, believed that they were following the example of Jesus who had withdrawn into the wilderness after his baptism (Luke 4.1–13). There, in the wilderness, Christians now sought the presence of God and the spiritual gift of holiness as they rejected any luxury and survived on the bare minimum and in individual prayer.

As they lived out their vows to live in poverty and constant prayer, these monks and nuns became renowned for their holiness, and often acquired large numbers of imitators and disciples, so that they became eagerly sought out for their wisdom and example – so much so that one early commentator, Athanasius, reported: 'The desert was made a city by all those monks who left their own people and enrolled for citizenship in heaven.' It was the beginning of the monastic movement, which was to give so much support and life to the Christian faith by its undoubted dedication and inspiration.

The desire of the desert fathers and mothers of this period, as they became known, was to search deep within their own souls for God's grace, and the discovery of the divine light at work in their inner being. They gave themselves to intense disciplines and sought to achieve the literal fulfilment of St Paul's exhortation: 'Pray without ceasing' (1 Thessalonians 5.17). The search for interior enlightenment became such a major movement that by the fifteenth century, those who practised its discipline took a specific name – they were hesychasts, from the Greek word meaning 'to be quiet', as they sought to still the very depths of their being, and to become aware of 'the uncreated light'.

The picture that heads this chapter is of John Climacus, otherwise known as St John of the Ladder, a sixth-century saint, who was one of the early exponents of inner quiet and constant prayer. He wrote a book, *The Ladder of Divine Ascent*, which quickly became a classic manual of spirituality, breaking down the discipline of the inner life into thirty steps. John enumerated and described in a practical way the qualities needed for the ascetic life. He wrote about how to build virtue and overcome vice.

The picture that I have included in this chapter is based upon ancient icons of John which depict him wearing the simple cowl or hood which became over time the accepted sign of the monastic vocation, and which is worn by many monks, especially of Eastern Christianity, to this day.

One distinctive prayer, which was developed by those, like John, who wanted to pray constantly, was a simple double phrase that could be prayed in a single complete breath cycle. Known as the Jesus Prayer, it is based on scripture, combining the confession of St Peter ('You are the Christ, the Son of the living God', in Matthew 16.16), and the prayer of the penitent tax collector ('God, be merciful to me, a sinner' in Luke 18.13), drawing upon the example of the repeated cry of Bartimaeus ('Son of David, have mercy on me', in Mark 10.47).

> Lord Jesus Christ, Son of the living God,
> Have mercy on me, a sinner.

Thoroughly scriptural, the Jesus Prayer in its simplicity is easily remembered and designed for repeated use, breath being slowly drawn in as the words 'Lord Jesus Christ, Son of [the living] God' are recited mentally, and exhaled during the words 'have mercy on me, a sinner'.

In one sense, this single prayer captures the entire gospel message, proclaiming Jesus as our Lord, and inviting his mercy on the person praying. The intention is to use the prayer so regularly and intensely that it becomes second nature, breathed and lived almost sub-consciously. The greatest exponents of the Jesus Prayer, such as the nineteenth-century Russian saint St Seraphim of Sarov, taught that by the discipline of this prayer, little by little a revelation of God's divine light would dawn over the soul.

Today, there are many Christians of both the East and the West who find the Jesus Prayer of enormous help in their spiritual lives. Requiring very little by way of intellectual comprehension, attentive reading or conscious composition, it is nonetheless demanding since it requires focus until there is an unconscious adoption in which simply breathing and praying are intimately connected. It is a prayer that focuses our attention on Jesus, and enables the heart to open up to God's grace.

> Lord Jesus Christ, Son of the living God,
> Have mercy on me, a sinner.

TEN

VENANTIUS FORTUNATUS
Sing, My Tongue

You could be forgiven for being a little shocked by the change of style in the illustration heading this chapter. This is because, with the exception of my portrait of King David, all the pictures so far have been based upon traditional icons of the relevant holy person, drawing broadly upon the Byzantine style of icon painting. With Venantius however, we are fortunate enough to have inherited a very early portrait of the great poet and hymn writer at work.

In an eleventh-century manuscript, Venantius is shown sitting at his desk composing a hymn, with parchment and ink before him, holding in his hands a reed pen and the knife that was used to trim the nib, and which could also act as a practical eraser for mistakes inscribed on the surface of vellum or goatskin, which was used for its durability and relative cheapness at a time when paper was rare. My picture is adapted from the portrait in this French manuscript which is kept in the municipal library in Poitiers, France, and deliberately reflects the style of the original Romanesque artwork. The portrait of Venantius appears in the work because he is the original author of one of the texts that makes up the bulk of the manuscript, his 'Life of St Radegund'. Radegund was a noblewoman belonging to the Merovingian royal family who ruled France and Germany from Metz during Venantius' lifetime, and was a significant patron of his work. Venantius in due time became the court poet to the Merovingian dynasty, although this did not prevent in turn his ordination as deacon, priest and bishop, signified in this portrait by his adoption of a tonsure, and ultimately his canonisation as a saint.

Eleven volumes of Latin poetry by Venantius have survived to the present day, offering compositions and poetry across sacred and secular themes. Many of his poems are in honour of the Merovingian kings, but he also cleverly wrote poems with a deeper agenda and intended to have a political impact, such as the poem that extravagantly praises the mercy of King Chilperic at a time when Venantius' friend and colleague Gregory of Tours was on trial for his life.

Venantius is in this book of prayers because he was a prolific hymn writer, at a time when music and Latin poetry were beginning to feature heavily in the worship of the Western Christian Church. In fact, Venantius composed two of the most famous early Christian hymns, which are still widely sung. These are known by their Latin names, the *Vexilla Regis* (The banners of the King) and the *Pange Lingua* (Sing, my tongue). Both these hymns praise God's love revealed in the Cross, and glorify the

Atonement, by which God in Christ won the redemption of humanity through his suffering and death.

Venantius' poetry puts Christ's sacrifice firmly back at the centre of our Christian faith, together with the Sacrament of Holy Communion, in which our lives and Christ's are linked by grace, and we feed sacramentally on the body and blood of Jesus, his gift to us (John 6.51).

As we enter into our own prayer, we can adopt the words and the hymns of Venantius, a thousand years old now, and we are encouraged to reflect on the mystery of the Incarnation, by which God was born as a child, lived among us, and then gave himself as a sacrifice to win our redemption. Venantius invites us to rise above the constraints of time, and to become witnesses to the historical reality of God entering into our midst in Jesus, and of the mysteries of the Incarnation, the Passion and the Holy Eucharist, which transcend chronology. These things surpass our understanding, and defy explanation – we are invited to accept them by faith, and join our prayers with those of this Latin poet in his words.

> Sing, my tongue, the Saviour's glory,
> Of his flesh, the mystery sing:
> Of the blood, all price exceeding,
> Shed by our immortal King,
> Destined, for the world's redemption,
> From a grace-filled womb to spring.
>
> On the night of that Last Supper,
> Seated with his chosen band,
> He, the Paschal Lamb consuming,
> First fulfilled the Law's command.
> Then, as food for all his brethren
> Gives himself with his own hand.

To Begetter and Begotten,
Praise and jubilation be,
Greeting, honour, strength and blessing,
And Salvation be set free.
To the One from both proceeding,
Equal praise and glory be.

(Adapted from a translation by Edward Caswall, 1814–78)

ELEVEN

MOZARABIC LITURGY
An Epiphany Prayer

The style of the picture heading this chapter is even more distinctive than the last. It is adapted from a picture that appears in a liturgical book of the Mozarabic tradition. The name Mozarabic is given to the culture of the Spanish Christians who continued their faith after the Muslim conquest of Spain in the eighth century. They had been developing a distinctive pattern of prayer and worship from the seventh century on, but became even more divorced from the mainstream European Christian culture as they became cut off politically as well as culturally. Mozarabic art and liturgy embody a fresh and primitive style, and continues to offer a distinct perspective on Christian life and prayer down to this day, especially through the life of the Spanish Reformed Episcopal Church.

The picture is drawn from an illustration in a Commentary on the Book of Revelation by Beatus of Liébana, and is part of one of over a hundred miniatures which appear in the manuscript, kept today in the National Library of Spain. Beatus was a notable theologian of the ninth century, and managed to maintain some correspondence with theologians from all over Europe including Alcuin of York, one of the greatest scholars at the court of Charlemagne. The illumination shows Christ returning in triumph at the end of the world, coming as 'the Son of Man' on the clouds of heaven, although it is hard to know in the illustration whether Jesus is depicted with the most incredible flowing locks of hair, or whether these should be understood as elements of the clouds of heaven. Beatus himself in his writings gave pre-eminence to the reading and interpretation of scripture, because, through Scripture, he believed, we encounter the living presence of Christ himself.

Because the liturgical books of the Mozarabic Christians survive, the prayers recorded in them give us a glimpse into the worship of Christians in this part of the world at this time. In these early centuries, there was much less standardisation of liturgy. Books were extremely expensive to create and to copy, so resources tended to remain local and isolated, even if scholars took care to correspond over vast distances which could be challenging even today.

In this period across Christendom, there are many prayers that reflect the growing practice of the Christian world of observing the liturgical year, linking the events of the revelation of God in Christ to specific dates and times. Easter was the first and obvious event to become associated with a particular time of year, given that it was possible to demonstrate the link between the crucifixion of Christ and the celebration of the

Jewish Passover. Even this was not as easy as it seems however, because the Jewish faith uses a lunar calendar, which does not align easily to the solar calendar with which we are so familiar. As time went on, the Annunciation to Mary of the birth of Jesus was linked symbolically to the beginning of the world, a date that was traditionally placed in the spring, and this led automatically to the placing of Christmas, the celebration of the birth of Christ, in December, nine months after the time attributed to the beginning of Mary's pregnancy.

The prayer that I have chosen to represent this stream of Christian life and devotion is a composition that scholars date to the seventh century. It is a prayer for the celebration of the Feast of the Epiphany, a season linked with Christmas by virtue of its theme of the revelation of Jesus Christ. The Church associated three events in the Gospels with the Epiphany: the visit of the magi, Jesus' baptism by John the Baptiser, and the first miracle at the wedding at Cana of Galilee, when Jesus turned water into wine. By far the most popular, however, proved to be the link with the visit of the Wise Men (or magi), and this is reflected in the prayer below by the mention of the light of the star, which went before the magi as they were guided to Jesus.

As we pray this prayer, we may give thanks for the differing ways in which the peoples of the world have received the good news of Christ in the Gospel, and for the myriad expressions of prayer and praise to which this has given birth. As the magi were representatives of all the nations of the world bringing their gifts to Jesus, so, in all cultures, the revelation of Jesus and the praise of God in Christ may be celebrated.

The heavens shine with the clear beauty of the stars, O Lord, and the earth itself is made beautiful by a shining light, because you undertook to appear to the world coming forth from your holy dwelling place.

Remove all sadness from our hearts, for you have come among us to make all things new.

Grant the same light that enlightened the eyes of your servants to enlighten our own eyes, to purify us and prepare us to behold you for ever; so that we, in preaching to the nations the glad joys of your appearing, may in time be made glad with you in infinite joy. Amen.

TWELVE

THE GELASIAN
SACRAMENTARY

An Evening Prayer

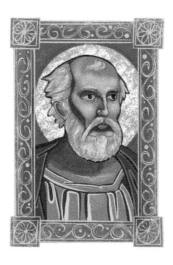

The picture associated with this chapter is based upon a mosaic disc displayed in the Basilica of St John Lateran, the Cathedral of Rome. High in the nave of the basilica, a series of discs offer a portrait of each of the popes from Peter to the present day. Gelasius I was pope between 492 and 496, and had gained a reputation for holiness and for a ministry as pope which had given order and structure to the worship conducted in the Roman Church. His memory was much cherished, and he therefore became a great role model in later ages and an authority for the future development of liturgy.

By the eighth century, there was a move to standardise the

prayers and worship in all the churches across Europe. The power and influence of the first Western Emperor of the Holy Roman Empire, Charlemagne, and the stability he had brought to European life, were hugely important in supplying a context by which the churches could be in regular communication and learn from one another.

At the same time, the Bishops of Rome were accumulating authority in the West, and Pope Gregory at the turn of the seventh century had been one of the first to send out collections of liturgical texts to be used at the celebration of the Eucharist. These books were known as Sacramentaries, and deposited with the chapels at the main royal courts with which he had correspondence. One such early sacramentary was attributed to the authorship of Pope Gelasius, although almost certainly his name was added later to give the prayers in it the apparent authority of ancient use and papal mandate. The Gelasian Sacramentary nevertheless remains as an important witness for us to the prayer of Christians in the eighth century, and provides a rich source of material.

The prayer that I have chosen from this collection is a prayer intended to be offered at evening. Very quickly, the custom had become established among Christians to offer prayer at the beginning and evening of each day, and before the Christian retired to bed for the night. Not unsurprisingly, the lighting of the lamps at dusk was a particular focus for prayer, connected richly with scripture. Over the centuries the pattern of prayer was elaborated, so that there came to be seven points of the day associated with prayer, reflecting the verse in the Book of Psalms, 'seven times a day I will praise you' (Psalm 119.164). Most of these were short services linked to a specific time – prime, terce, sext or none (the first, third, sixth and ninth hour) – but these were linked with the more major services of Mattins (Morning Prayer), Vespers (Evening Prayer) and Compline (Night Prayer).

Like many Christian words of worship, the prayer for the evening chosen below has a close link with the Bible. Jesus had told a famous parable (Matthew 25.1–13) comparing the people of God to the attendants of a bride at her wedding. It was the custom for friends of the bride and relatives of the groom to await the arrival of the bride at the groom's residence, since the groom would bring his new wife from the home of her parents to his own home after the formal wedding ceremony. This would often be late at night, since wedding parties continued then as now late into the evening. Guests and bridesmaids at the receiving home would have to wait until the unscheduled arrival of the bridal party. Jesus used this scenario as a parable of God's kingdom. The kingdom would be inaugurated by the triumphant arrival of the Messiah, the Christ, but it would come suddenly and unexpectedly, in the manner of a bridal party. The wise – those who listened to Jesus' warnings of the way in which God's kingdom would come – would be prepared like bridesmaids who had their lamps prepared, keeping stocks of extra oil to keep them alight for many hours, and trimming the wicks to ensure that the flame did not gutter.

The prayer draws as well on a verse in Paul's Letter to the Philippians (2.14–15): 'Do all things without grumbling or disputing, that you may be blameless and innocent, children of God without blemish in the midst of a crooked and twisted generation, among whom you shine as lights in the world.'

Generous God, fulfil our desire
and kindle our hearts by your Spirit,
that being filled with the oil of your grace,
we may shine as bright lights at the coming
of your Son Jesus Christ;
who lives and reigns with you and the Holy Spirit,
one God, now and for ever. Amen.

THIRTEEN
RABANUS MAURUS
Veni Creator

As the liturgies of the Church evolved, so there grew up along-side the scriptures and psalms a corpus of 'hymns', songs of praise not directly quoting scripture but addressed to God, and drawing the worshipper into the adoration of God. One of the earliest and most famous is the 'Te Deum', a hymn going back possibly to St Ambrose or St Augustine in the fourth century. Pliny the Younger, a Roman governor of the turn of the second century, had written to the Emperor Trajan for advice about how to handle the early Christians, and had quoted their habits of worship: 'They are accustomed to meet on a fixed day before dawn and sing responsively a hymn to Christ as to a god.' As we have noted, the use of music was widespread in Christian worship, drawing, as it did, on the tradition established by the psalms, which refer to their setting with the use of psaltery, harps and trumpets.

We have already met Venantius Fortunatus, one of the great hymn writers of the sixth century, and today's chapter focuses upon Rabanus Magnentius, one of the great hymn writers of the ninth century. Rabanus was originally a Benedictine monk in Fulda in Germany, and an inheritor of the formidable cultural legacy of the court of Charlemagne. There he had been taught by the great scholar Alcuin, who gave him the nickname 'Maurus' after the favourite disciple of St Benedict, to reflect the student teacher relationship between Alcuin and Rabanus. Rabanus was an apt pupil and destined for great things: he went on to become Archbishop of Mainz in 847. The portrait at the head of this chapter is taken from a twelfth century volume compiled in the Abbey at Anchin, and now kept in the public Library of Douai in France. It shows Rabanus dedicating his book of hymns to Pope Gregory, the pope of the sixth century, who had worked alongside Venantius Fortunatus.

Rabanus composed one of the greatest hymns in Christian history, which is still widely used to this day: '*Veni, Creator Spiritus*'. We have already noted the centrality to Christian belief of the revelation of God as Trinity. This is the belief that an infinite and unknowable God has chosen to reveal himself as Three in One, Father, Son and Holy Spirit. The Father is the prime source of all creation, who revealed himself to the people of Israel in the revelation in history recorded in the Tanakh (the Torah, Prophets and Writings that make up the volume that Christians refer to as the Old Testament). For Christians, of course, the complete revelation of God's person and nature was given in the person of Jesus, God incarnate among us, but there is also the abiding presence of God in the world, the Spirit, sent from the Father in response to the prayer of the Son (John 14.16).

Rabanus' great hymn calls upon the Holy Spirit to guide and protect the faithful Christian in life, and the hymn is therefore recognised as the most appropriate chant for ordinations or confirmations, occasions when the Holy Spirit is invited to strengthen the life of the Church, its clergy and those joining the Church family. To this day, it is often sung in a plainsong form, without instrumental accompaniment, and with great effect, as the surrounding liturgy halts for the invocation of God's Spirit on proceedings.

There are many translations from the Latin in which Rabanus originally worked. The translation presented in this chapter was composed by Bishop John Cosin, the seventeenth-century Anglican Bishop of Durham. The hymn bears repeated use. As we pray it, we can perhaps invite the Holy Spirit to bless us in life, and illuminate for us the truth of the gospel, by which the Church has been led for twenty centuries.

> Come, Holy Ghost, our souls inspire
> and lighten with celestial fire;
> thou the anointing Spirit art,
> who dost thy sevenfold gifts impart.
>
> Thy blessed unction from above
> is comfort, life, and fire of love;
> enable with perpetual light
> the dullness of our mortal sight.
>
> Teach us to know the Father, Son,
> and thee, of both, to be but one;
> that through the ages all along
> this may be our endless song:
>
> Praise to thine eternal merit,
> Father, Son and Holy Spirit.
> Amen.

FOURTEEN
THE GREGORIAN SACRAMENTARY
A Pentecost Prayer

You will already have recognised from earlier chapters of this book the central place that the Bishops of Rome have had in the history of Western Christianity. Faced with the collapse of the Roman Empire of the West, the Bishops of Rome were freed from the power of the Roman emperors of the East now based at Constantinople, but, more than this, were left largely responsible for the political survival of Western Europe, and the life of faith and culture in the various societies formed by the barbarian invaders after the third century. One of the most successful of the popes of the early Middle Ages was Gregory the Great, as his title suggests. Gregory was a Roman citizen, who had had a distinguished career as a civil servant. Eventually he became a monk and retired from the world, but his skills could not be ignored, and he was suborned into a second distinguished career as a papal diplomat. Around the year 540, Gregory was elected as Pope himself. Blessed with a reforming zeal, Gregory set about putting the Western Church on a secure footing. Given that travel was not easy, the Pope used correspondence as a way of spreading and enforcing his views on the development of the Church; 854 of his letters survive to this day as well as many of his sermons and other writings.

The picture heading this chapter complements the earlier picture of Rabanus Maurus, and it is adapted from the same manuscript illumination, showing Pope Gregory receiving the dedication of Rabanus' works. The pope is perhaps most famous in the English speaking world for initiating the conversion of the English to Christianity. The story of the occasion when he encountered young English slaves in the markets of Rome, distinguished by their fair hair, is well known. Gregory enquired of their origin, and on being told, described them as 'Angels not Angles'. It was this encounter that inspired Gregory to commission Augustine, (not to be confused with the Augustine of Chapter 7, but the Prior of the Monastery of St Andrew in Rome), to lead a mission to England, which he undertook somewhat unwillingly.

Gregory was also recognised as one of the key figures bringing uniformity and high standards to the worship of the Western Church, as we have noted above. He is believed to be the prime editor of the surviving Liturgy of the Presanctified Gifts, still used in Orthodox Churches of the East for the period of Lent. He is also known as the person who established the use of plainchant as the main musical form deployed in Christian worship – so much so that it is sometimes known to this day as Gregorian Chant.

We should not be surprised therefore, that in the same manner of Pope Gelasius, many prayers and collections in the Sacramentaries of the medieval Church are attributed to Pope Gregory, and the prayer that I have chosen for this day comes from the 'Gregorian Sacramentary' which became the standard liturgical text for the Church in Europe, and which can be dated to the tenth century, five centuries after the life of the pope after whom it is named. Gregory developed the process by which standard biblical and eucharistic texts for Sunday worship were supplemented by a rich variety of collects (which are short prayers in a similar format, intended to be prayers drawing together the worship of the faithful) and which are developed as a set of special prayers for each Sunday and season of the Church's year. Although the book is therefore a later text, it probably draws on prayers which already had established antiquity when they were recorded, and so the ascription to Gregory may not be entirely spurious.

The example I have chosen is a collect for the Feast of Pentecost, and picks up on the work of Rabanus Maurus. The Holy Spirit is the person of God at work in the lives of Christian disciples today, and accessible to all believers. The prayer speaks of a threefold ministry of the Spirit in the hearts of the faithful – enlightening them with the truth, imparting the gift of wisdom so that disciples have the ability to make the right call in different and difficult situations, and requesting the comfort of the Spirit's power in all sorts of difficulties.

We are invited to pray for the ministry of the Holy Spirit in our own lives, and in the life of the Church in our own day. This is particularly needed in a time of great social change, when the Church has to make difficult judgements about how to accommodate new ideas in its life, and yet remain faithful in all essentials to the faith revealed in Jesus.

O God,
on this day you taught the hearts of your faithful people
by sending them the light of your Holy Spirit.
Give us a right judgment in all things
by the power of that same Spirit
that we may always rejoice in his holy comfort;
through your Son, Jesus Christ our Lord,
who with you and the Holy Spirit lives and reigns,
one God, now and forever. Amen.

FIFTEEN

THE BOOK OF TALIESIN
On the Face of the Earth

It will have become obvious to readers that sacred tradition is an important part of the history of Christian prayer. Later prayers and collections are often attributed to earlier writers and saints; inspiration is found in their example and holiness, and a prayer may reflect on, or speak into, the experience and teaching of a saint who lived centuries before. From the liturgy of St Mark to the Sacramentaries of St Gregory, a tradition of lively intercessors is invoked. This is because Christianity believes that God's intention is clear. We should grow up into the fullness of a life that God sets out for each individual as we learn to inhabit the wholeness of God's plan for us. We should expect therefore to see 'saints', those made holy by the action of God's love in their lives, and who give us an example of how to follow Jesus in our own lives.

In the Celtic tradition of Wales, St David is such a figure. A saint of the 'Age of Saints' in the sixth century, David was the founder and abbot of the monastery of Mynyw. Here, he became famous for his austerity, subsisting on a diet of root vegetables, and subjecting himself to hard disciplines of prayer and fasting. He drank nothing but water, earning himself the sobriquet of 'David the water-drinker' in the later annals of the Welsh saints. His holiness was renowned, and the final charge that he offered to his monks as he approached his own death has become famous: 'My lords, my brothers and sisters, be joyful and keep to your faith and to your creed. Do the little things that you have heard about from me and seen me do. As for me, I will walk the path taken by our fathers.' Remembered for this practical advice, David became the patron saint of Wales, and the archetype of the Welsh Celtic tradition.

The icon at the head of this chapter is my interpretation of a modern icon of David, showing him in his monastic habit, and holding the book of the faith that he kept, and which he is said to have defended with vigour at the important Synod of Llanddewi Brefi.

In later centuries, there exist a number of collections of prayers which take their inspiration from the Age of Saints, and hold close to the tradition that God is revealed and apprehended in his creation. In the Book of Taliesin, named after an ancient Welsh bard, there is a collection of remembered Welsh tales, poems and prayers. The book itself dates from the early fourteenth century, but is a collection of much older oral traditions. Sandwiched between two poems about Alexander the Great (who was understood to be the archetype of what a great hero looked like in medieval legend), there is a prayer in the tradition of the lorica prayers explained in the chapter on Patrick (Chapter 8). This particular prayer is believed to date from the eleventh century, and reflects on the revelation of God in Jesus, and the healing and redemption that he wrought in his earthly life. I have chosen this prayer as a representative of the Welsh tradition of prayer, and invite us to make it our own.

On the face of the earth, no equal has been born.
Of three persons in God, in the almighty Trinity,
he is the gentle Son.
Son of God, and Son of Man,
he is the One true and wonderful Son.
As Son of God, he is a fortress,
As Son of the blessèd Mary, he is lovely to behold.
Of the race of Adam and Abraham he was born,
Of the people of God, in the line of the eloquent psalmist.
By a word he freed the blind and the deaf from their ailments;
And even a vain people, iniquitous and perverse,
can be raised in the sight of the Trinity by his redemption.
For the Cross of Christ is our shining breastplate
against every injury,
And in every hardship, here is our city of refuge.

SIXTEEN

FRANCIS OF ASSISI

Make Me a Channel of your Peace

The title of this chapter is a bit of a fraud. Sadly, the popular hymn widely known as 'The Prayer of St Francis' was not written by the saint at all, and has no known connection to him. It was first published in French in 1910 in a magazine called 'La Clochette', *The Little Bell*, which disseminated prayers and reflections, but in it, that prayer is unattributed. While this is a disappointment, Francis did leave authentic writings, and was in fact the author of many works, including a famous Canticle, in which Francis celebrates his relationship with all the elements of creation, and joins them in praising God. This affinity with creation, and his obvious love and concern for nature, have won Francis many admirers in the present day when eco-logical concerns feature high on people's agendas. Indeed, Pope John Paul II declared Francis the patron saint of ecology in 1979. However, Francis also won much admiration in earlier centuries for his complete rejection of worldly wealth and status, and the poverty and generosity to others which became his hallmark.

The picture offered in this chapter is based upon an early portrait of Francis in the Basilica in Assisi named after him. The portrait was painted by the great Renaissance Italian painter Cimabué, and is reputedly a good likeness. I like it because it captures something of the unruly and mischievous nature of Francis, a character who won admirers and followers among the people as easily in life as he offended those who were rich and powerful.

Francis was born in the twelfth century, the son of a wealthy merchant, and was baptised and given the name Giovanni by his mother, only receiving his more famous nickname from his father, who called him 'Frenchy'. Although his father had many links with France, and was believed to be away in France when Francis was born, the real reason for this famous nickname is lost to history. A typical teenager, Francis enjoyed life to the full, although on one occasion he gave away his entire earnings to a beggar on whom he took pity, much to the amazement of his friends, and to his father's disgust. In 1205, he had the first of a series of visions, and adopted the life of a beggar himself, but not before he had given away a lot of the profits of his father's business.

Attracted by the story of the way in which Jesus commis-sioned his disciples (Matthew 10), Francis sought to follow Jesus' teaching, espousing poverty and seeking to do good for those in need around him. Very early on, others joined him and became the core of the future Order of Friars Minor, better known as the Franciscans. There must have been something highly attractive in Francis, because not only did he win a large number of dedicated followers, but Pope Innocent III readily offered the emergent order his patronage, and Cardinal Ugolino di Conti, an influential member of the papal court, became the order's mentor.

Francis remained the provocateur he had been in his youth, travelling to Egypt during the Fifth Crusade, and crossing enemy lines to visit the Sultan and preaching to him. He became famous for many things – setting up the first ever Christmas nativity scene, and on one notable occasion even preaching to the birds. However, throughout his life, Francis remained dedicated to the vision of poverty that had inspired his ministry, living and dying in simplicity. Ugolino di Conti, his old friend, was elected Pope as Gregory IX in 1227, and one of his first acts was formally to declare Francis a saint.

The challenge of Francis' poverty is one that most of us cannot match, although his vision of a simple life should teach us to sit lightly to possessions. His ready embrace of creation as an extension of his being, and his belief in the unity of all God's creation, are ideas that we can embrace in our own faith and which are very timely in today's world. Even more timely, at a time when death is rarely a topic for polite conversation, is Francis' assertion that physical death is a natural part of the cycle of life, and is not to be feared. So we can pray with Francis:

O most high, almighty and good Lord,
To you belong all praise and glory, honour and blessing.
Be praised, my Lord, by all your creation,
Especially Brother Sun, who brings the day,
and gives us light through him.

Be praised, O Lord, by Sister Moon, and all the stars,
For you created them in the heavens,
clear and precious and beautiful.

Be praised, O Lord, by Brother Wind, by air and cloud,
in all times and weather,
Through which all your creatures are sustained.
Be praised, O Lord, by Sister Water, useful and humble,
precious and chaste.
Be praised by Brother Fire, who lights the night,
playful, robust and strong.
Be praised by Sister Mother Earth,
who sustains us and governs us,
And brings forth fruits, bright coloured flowers and herbs.

Be praised, O Lord, by the life of those who forgive
because of your love,
Who bear with infirmity or tribulation.
For blessed are those who endure in peace,
And by you, O Most High, they will be crowned.

Be praised, O Lord, by Sister Death,
From whom there is no escape,
But blessed are those who treasure your holy will,
For the second death shall do them no harm.

SEVENTEEN

CLARE OF ASSISI
A Prayer of Blessing

One of the earliest followers of Francis was another resident of
Assisi, Clare Offreduccio. As a teenager, Clare heard Francis
preaching, and was inspired to seek him out after the service,
and ask how best she could live in response to his vision of
Christian discipleship. On Palm Sunday, 1212, with the consent
of the local bishop, Clare, accompanied by her aunt Bianca,
and another friend, met with Francis in a local chapel. There,
Clare made vows under his direction to lead a life of simplicity.
Francis placed Clare in the care of the local Benedictine nuns
of San Paulo, Bastia, but her family were less convinced of
her vocation, and attempted to rescue her by force from the

community. It is said that Clare resisted by clinging to the pillars surrounding the altar in the convent church, and that it was only when her veil fell off during the struggle, and the family saw how she had cropped her hair, that they began to realise how serious Clare's decision was. Indeed, so impressive was her commitment that her sister, Catarina, joined her within the fortnight, a turn of events that was unlikely have increased the joy of the family.

Eventually, the friars built a small convent building next to the Church of San Damiano, one of Francis' favourite churches, to house the growing community of religious sisters, who together became known as 'the Poor Ladies of San Damiano'. In the same way that the Franciscans had grown rapidly, many women joined the Poor Ladies, and San Damiano quickly became the centre of the 'Second Order of St Francis', an order for women, eventually called the 'Poor Clares' because of their absolute commitment to live in poverty and austerity, which they believed was the true way to follow the example set by Jesus.

While Francis lived, his reputation and support protected Clare and her community, but, after his death in 1226, Clare faced a challenge from the Church. Many, although sympathetic, felt that the sisters were taking poverty too seriously, to the extent that they were risking their health. The sisters went barefoot, slept on the ground, ate a vegetarian diet and kept almost complete silence, as they devoted themselves to the example of Jesus. Among those who feared for their well-being was the same Ugolino di Conti who was a friend of both Francis and Clare. As Pope Gregory IX, Ugolino visited Clare in Assisi and argued with her to adopt a more measured lifestyle for herself and her sisters. 'If you feel bound by your vows,' he is said to have stated to Clare, 'then I, as Pope, herewith dispense you from those vows.' Clare's answer was equally direct: 'Holy

Father, I would never wish in any way to be dispensed from following Christ.' The pope recognised that he was beaten, and approved a charter for the Second Order.

The picture of Clare in this chapter is adapted from another fresco in the Basilica in Assisi, this time by the great painter Giotto. It shows Clare in the simple habit that she and her sisters adopted, a black veil which was worn over the simple undyed and course brown cloth worn by all Franciscans.

The example of both Francis and Clare was revolutionary in their own day, and triggered a revival of religious life and discipleship of Jesus. There is something both inspiring and shocking about their dedication and determination to live in absolute poverty, harking back to the example of Jesus, who had no place to lay his head (Matthew 8.20), and the apostles who shared out all their possessions to the whole community (Acts 4.32) and eschewed the ownership of money (Acts 3.6). It is a far cry from the comfort in which most Christians of the developed world live, and I believe that we are all called to reflect on the extent of our possessions, and how we answer God's call in our lives. Perhaps we have to be honest, and admit that we are half-hearted disciples, and if we can be kind to ourselves, we ought to be kind when tempted to judge the level of Christian commitment that we see in others.

The later letters of the Bible, sometimes known as the Pastoral Epistles, wrangle with the fact that many disciples of the early Church brought wealth with them into their life of faith. The Letter of James is a good example. The writer acknowledges differences of wealth in this world, and admonishes his readers that all material wealth is transitory. Equality is one of the marks of the coming kingdom of God, and James urges his readers to use their wealth in a way that embodies a generous attitude towards others, and which advances economic justice.

Wealth is a double-edged gift, and brings a responsibility to sit lightly to comfort and use our resources for the good of others.

Clare wrote a blessing for her community, which is the prayer adopted for this chapter. Clare calls us to faithfulness for our profession of faith and our commitment to live as disciples of Jesus. Whatever our decision and commitment about wealth, Clare calls us to be confident in our faith, ready to move forward, but with a lightness in our purpose. It speaks both of our faith, and of our action, and our readiness to move forward in faith.

What you hold may you always hold.
What you do, may you always do and never abandon.
But with a swift pace, a light step and unswerving feet,
so that even your steps stir up no dust,
Go forward, the Spirit of our God has called you.

EIGHTEEN

RICHARD OF CHICHESTER
Day by Day

Francis' Canticle of the Sun was made famous by the film of his life, directed by Franco Zefirelli, *Brother Sun, Sister Moon*. In the same way, one of the prayers of St Richard of Chichester was made famous by a version sung in the 1970s theatre hit, *Godspell*.

Richard became Bishop of Chichester in the south of England between 1244 and 1253. He had risen through the ranks of the clergy as a teacher and theologian, teaching at each of the three great medieval universities of Oxford, Paris and Bologna. Having been ordained to the priesthood in 1242, he was elected as Bishop of Chichester in 1244, although a dispute with King

Henry III over his election delayed his assumption of the See for a further year. Living an austere life himself, he upheld high standards among the clergy, reforming their moral conduct, and insisting on reverence and decency in worship. By the time that he died in 1253, he was widely acknowledged as a holy man, and very quickly miracles were reported to have occurred at his tomb.

One story, which shows the seriousness with which Richard approached worship, relates to an incident that occurred while he was celebrating the Eucharist. As he consecrated the bread and the wine at the high altar in Chichester Cathedral, a spider is said to have fallen from the rafters into the chalice containing the consecrated wine. Spiders were widely considered as poisonous in the medieval period, and to consume one was to die. Richard, however, faithful to his priestly duties, knew that the sacred wine had to be consumed, spider and all, and accepted the challenge. Having downed the spider, he is said to have returned to his stall and prepared himself for death.

The image that heads this chapter is a version of the picture of St Richard based upon a modern icon by Sergei Fyodorov, the original of which is in Chichester Cathedral. Many icon designs have been passed down the generations for centuries, and it is the task of the iconographer to replicate tradition, and not to innovate. As icons have become popular in the West, however, there are saints now being depicted for which there is no standard inherited image, and innovation and tradition have to be woven together to create new models for future iconographers.

The famous prayer which bears Richard's name, was first faithfully recorded by his chronicler, and has been in frequent use down to today. It is said originally to have been fashioned from his last words upon his death bed, although sadly the famous triplet at the end of the prayer is not attested until the twentieth century. The first part of the original prayer contains a reference to scripture, and to the first chapter of the Book of Lamentations, which was understood by commentators as prophetic words addressed as if by Christ to those passing by the crucifixion:

'Is it nothing to you, all you who pass by?
Look and see if there is any sorrow like my sorrow,
which was brought upon me,
which the LORD inflicted on the day of his fierce anger.'

(Lamentations 1.12)

St Richard's prayer constitutes a great example of how a prayer changes and mutates over time – how it is worn smooth into the shape that best helps people's faith. The core of any good prayer is remembered and re-used, but some phrases are forgotten and others added as Christians build their own devotion around the core idea, contributing their own insights and petitions.

The original prayer speaks more of Richard's gratitude for the hope of salvation, which fits the context originally given, while the modern version puts the emphasis on ongoing discipleship. To be a follower of Jesus is not just an occasional activity, but it must be transformative of the whole of life. Nevertheless, such a task is the endeavour of a whole lifetime, and not achieved all at once.

As we pray this prayer, it urges us to push on with our own discipleship, and to look to make progress perhaps in little ways 'day by day', words that appear to have been added to the prayer in a hymnal of 1933.

Thanks be to you, my Lord Jesus Christ,
For all the blessings you have given me,
For all the pains and insults you have endured for me,
On which account you offered this cry:
'Behold, and see, if there is any sorrow like my sorrow.'
O merciful redeemer, my friend and brother,
May I know you more clearly,
Love you more dearly, and
Follow you more nearly,
This day and every day. Amen.

NINETEEN

CATHERINE OF SIENA
A Prayer of Devotion

Catherine is one of the greatest woman saints of the fourteenth century. Born in Siena, her life follows a pattern familiar from Clare (Chapter 17), and she became devoted to the Christian faith from an early age, and sought to enter religious life. She joined a community of women associated with the Dominican order, an order that has always been widely known for its scholarship, and devoted herself to helping those who were ill or in prison – following the counsel of Jesus (Matthew 25.35–36).

Throughout her life, Catherine experienced a series of visions, including one in which she saw herself as united with Jesus in a spiritual marriage. When she was twenty-eight, she received a vision in which Christ appeared to her and asked her to choose between a crown of gold and jewels, ensuring riches in her earthly life, or a crown of thorns, which meant suffering in this world, but glory in the world to come. Her choice became clear to all from her manner of life, and Catherine is often shown wearing a crown of thorns as a result of her own account of this vision. This is reflected in the picture chosen for this chapter, which is an adaptation of an early portrait of Catherine, painted by the Italian artist Andrea Vanni.

Such visions seem strange to the modern mind, but the impact of Catherine's visions manifested themselves in her life commitments to a gracious and holy life wholly given to helping the poor that she sought out in Siena. This practical outworking and commitment gives a certain authenticity to the fruitfulness of her visions and inner life. Even early on, Catherine became renowned as a holy woman, and this made her influential beyond Church life, and in local civic life. As a result, Catherine became involved in addressing the political tensions between Siena and Florence, becoming a strong advocate for peace at a time when the Italian cities were often in conflict. She was sent as part of the diplomatic team of Siena to neighbouring cities, where her passionate advocacy of peace was seen as a powerful force. From 1375 onwards, Catherine took up writing letters to political figures all over Europe, urging the Christian leaders of Europe to live by the precepts of their faith and to pursue peace. This ministry was recognised by a number of the popes, who used Catherine as an ambassador and diplomat.

In all these things, Catherine seems to have been driven by a deep conviction of the love of God for the world, and the response of love which this should elicit from his creation. She described in one of her letters how God was like the sea, and all humanity like fish that swam in his waters, dependent on his grace to live our lives. Her wisdom and direct tone were deeply valued in her lifetime, and have been remembered ever since – in 1970 Pope Paul VI recognised her as a Doctor of the Church: doctor meaning teacher, a title that is reserved to the most pre-eminent of theologians, such as Jerome and Augustine.

The qualities of Catherine, committed to an intense life of prayer which cannot be separated from a practical application in life, stand as an example to us all. The Scriptures teach us that any worthwhile faith will demonstrate itself in a radical commitment to changing the world for the better (James 2.18). For Catherine, everything was made possible by the love of Jesus for us. This prayer, adapted from her writings, invites us to draw close to God's love and protection, and asks God to enable us to go out as healers in the world.

Holy Spirit, come into my heart;
and draw me to you by your power, O my God.
Grant me love with childlike awe,
and preserve me, O beautiful love,
from every evil thought.
Warm me and inflame me with your great love,
So that every pain will seem light to me.
My Father, my sweet Lord, help me in all my actions.
Jesus, let us know your love, Jesus, let us know your love.
Amen.

TWENTY

POPE JOHN XXII
Anima Christi

We have already noted the high profile role adopted by the Popes as reformers of liturgy across the Western Church. By the medieval period, the role of the popes as Patriarchs of the Western Church and increasingly in Catholic theology, as Head of the Universal Church, were well established. In her letters, Catherine had addressed the Bishop of Rome as 'Bappo', 'Daddy', and the standard honorific of 'Father' had become the title par excellence of only two senior clerics – one in the West, and one in the East, the Pope of Rome and the Pope of Alexandria – titles that survive to this day.

Jacques Duèze, a Frenchman, was elected as Pope in 1316. It is highly likely that his election was assisted by the fact that the popes were currently living in exile from Rome, having been driven out of the eternal city by popular rebellions by the citizens, who aspired to the sort of freedoms experienced by other Italian cities like Siena and Florence. Under the influence of powerful French kings such as Philip IV, the popes set up their papal court at the French town of Avignon, and remained there for seventy years until able to return to Rome. Jacques took the name of John when he became Pope, following the tradition of selecting a new name, which had begun many centuries before. He was a notable theologian and teacher, having been Chancellor of the University of Avignon, and is credited with composing one of the most famous Christian prayers of all time – the 'Anima Christi'.

The picture that heads this chapter is based upon the sixteenth-century portrait by Giuseppe Franco which is kept as one of a series of the portraits of the popes in the Ambrosian Library in Milan, and shows the pope wearing early versions of the papal insignia, the pallium and the tiara, which is half mitre and half crown.

The 'Anima Christi' is a devotional prayer, often associated with the Eucharist, which invokes Christ's healing power through the sacramental gifts of water, bread and wine. Its focus upon God's saving work in Jesus has made it a ready source of devotion for centuries, often just before or after receiving Communion, and was a favourite prayer of Ignatius of Loyola (Chapter 23), and much used by him. In some ways, it harks back to the traditions of the lorica prayers (Chapters 8 and 15), since it invokes the power of God to protect us and nourish us in life, although its orientation is towards the Eucharistic celebration. People have found it a useful prayer in connection with the celebration of the Eucharist, as it almost provides a commentary and interpretation of what is understood to be God's action in the sacrament. The translation given below is based upon the translation of John Henry Newman made in the nineteenth century.

Christians believe that the two sacraments of baptism and communion were given directly by Jesus as effective signs and channels of his grace. He called us to receive him into our lives (John 14), and to be nourished with his sacramental presence (John 6.53). As we say this prayer, let us pray that we might draw near to Christ, and know his mercy in our lives. 'Let us then with confidence draw near to the throne of grace, that we may receive mercy and find grace to help in time of need' (Hebrews 4.16).

Soul of Christ: impart true holiness;
Christ's Body, with salvation bless;
Blood of Christ, fill all my veins;
Water from Christ's side: wash out all my stains.
Passion of Christ, my comfort be;
O good Jesus, be close to me;
In your wounds I wish to hide;
Never parted from your side;
Guard me, should the foe assail me;
Call me when my life shall fail me;
Bid me come to you above,
And with your saints to sing your love.
Amen.

TWENTY-ONE
THOMAS À KEMPIS
A Real Beginning

We who have lived through the Covid crisis of recent years have experienced a taste of what it is to live through a pandemic, and to see widespread deaths and bereavement. The shock to modern society has permanently altered the ways in which we relate, and life seems to have become slightly more fragile and slightly more frenetic ever since. Fortunately, medical science had developed in a way that enabled swift programmes of immunisation, and the impact of the virus was quickly lessened, and, to some extent, overcome.

This is as nothing to the shock that Europe faced in the mid-fourteenth century, when the Black Death swept across Europe and wiped out perhaps over a third of the population.

Society was dislocated, the old structures of feudalism which kept the peasantry in check were loosened, and there was greater freedom and social and economic mobility. There was also a shift in spirituality, as the fragility of human life before God was emphasised afresh, and people considered the way in which they needed to intercede for the mercy and compassion of God, and how their personal faith could give resilience and hope in life. There was a wave of new sponsorship for religious art and literature, and a growth in spiritual and emotional literacy. A new form of religious discipleship, the *Devotio Moderna*, took root, in which personal faith and piety were emphasised, and lay associations of the faithful emerged – both in the rise of commercial guilds, which were often centred on a particular church or saint, or confraternities who came together to facilitate growth in personal faith and mutual encouragement.

Of particular prominence in the fifteenth century were the Brethren of the Common Life, a religious dispersed community centred in the low countries (modern Belgium and the Netherlands), whose emphasis was on religion in everyday life and spiritual practices that depended on disciplines of personal prayer and inner devotion to God. They spoke of the four cornerstones of faith: contempt of the world and self, imitation of the humility of Christ, an attitude of good will to their neighbours, and seeking from God the grace to become devout.

Thomas à Kempis is probably the most famous exponent of the *Devotio Moderna*, encapsulated in his most influential work, *The Imitation of Christ*, a classic of Christian spirituality still widely read today. The sixteenth-century scholar and saint Sir Thomas More even recommended *The Imitation of Christ* as one of three books that every Christian should own and read, and the book was widely translated and disseminated following its first publication. Thomas à Kempis himself became a monk, and was eventually ordained as a priest. The picture heading this chapter is adapted from a contemporary portrait by an unknown artist, which captured his humanity and good humour.

The Imitation of Christ is a down to earth handbook of how to live a Christian life of prayer and faithfulness in following Jesus. It consisted of four pamphlets written by Thomas which were then bound together to make one book. The first section, 'Helpful Counsels for the Spiritual Life', stressed the importance of finding space for solitude and silence as a context for prayer, and offered simple guidance on how to pray. The second section, 'Directives for the Inner Life', spoke about the importance of peace in the inner being, purity of heart and a good conscience, while the third was written in the form of a dialogue between Christ and a typical disciple – a sort of early FAQs. Finally, the fourth section spoke of the importance of the sacraments, through which the grace of God can infuse and animate the life of the disciple.

I am particularly fond of the humanity and practicality of Thomas' faith and teaching. It is less about judgement and wrath, and more about discovering how God can be at work in our hearts. One prayer from *The Imitation of Christ* has spoken to me from the beginning of my own discipleship in my youth. Thomas acknowledges our desire to walk the path of discipleship, but also knows that the fragility of our response means that progress is slow and not likely to be all progress. Nevertheless, the heart can be open before God admitting that fragility and seeking for the grace to grow stronger. It was therefore a prayer that appealed to me, as a prayer with which I could begin each day. I hope that it is a prayer in which you can join me:

> Help me, O God, in my good resolutions,
> and in your holy service,
> and grant that this day I may make a good beginning,
> for until now I have done hardly anything!

TWENTY-TWO

THOMAS CRANMER
A Prayer of Humble Access

Coupled with the new atmosphere of intellectual inquiry and personal freedom that followed the Black Death, the advent of printing in Europe suddenly facilitated books like *The Imitation of Christ*. Printing literally put books into the hands of thousands rather than those who had privileged access to the manuscripts stored in secluded libraries, which belonged to the era when books were so costly to copy and reproduce. By the beginning of the sixteenth century, we see the emergence of Humanism as an intellectual movement – not the modern secular humanism, which denies the place of faith or the supernatural, but an emphasis on the quality of the human mind and the power of reason. Humanism also drew on the inheritance of human culture from ancient times onwards, on the established fruits of classical philosophy and the new harvest of scientific enquiry. Scholars like Erasmus offered a critique of traditional understandings of religion and salvation, by going back to the Bible and re-interpreting the teaching of Jesus, drawing on the original Greek texts rather than the Latin Vulgate, while various movements challenged the religious establishment.

In 1517, a loud-mouthed and passionate Theology lecturer at Wittenberg University in Germany challenged the papal practice of selling indulgences offering release from the pains of purgatory in return for a cash donation to the rebuilding of St Peter's Basilica in Rome. Martin Luther started a religious avalanche that blew apart the religious consensus of the medieval period, and triggered what scholars know as the Reformation, which rejected the authority of human hierarchies and the popes, and called for a radical revisioning of Christianity based solely on the Bible.

In 1529, a rising scholar of Cambridge University was appointed as Archdeacon of Taunton, and sent off to the continent on various diplomatic missions. His name was Thomas Cranmer, and he was quickly recognised by King Henry VIII as a source of wisdom and fresh thinking. Henry appointed Cranmer as Archbishop of Canterbury when the opportunity arose in 1532, and this position put Cranmer at the helm of religious life in England. Unbeknown to the King, Cranmer had already become influenced by Lutheran ideas and religion, and had even married Margarete, the niece of the Protestant reformer Andreas Osiander, breaking the medieval pattern of clerical celibacy.

The sixteenth century saw the true emergence of personal portraiture as an art, and there are a couple of well-attested portraits of Thomas Cranmer. The picture offered in this chapter is adapted from a sixteenth-century portrait of Cranmer towards the end of his life; it was painted shortly after his martyrdom and is kept at Lambeth Palace, home of the Archbishops of Canterbury. It is by an unknown artist, but offers a chance to encounter Thomas in a lifelike manner, not easily available for earlier generations. It is said that Thomas grew his beard long as a sign of mourning on Henry VIII's death, and as a mark of his commitment to reform.

With the succession of Edward VI, Henry's only legitimate son, in 1547, Cranmer found himself charged with the task of composing new liturgies in English for the Church of England, which now identified itself with the main principles of the continental reformers. Drawing on the help of a wide range of scholars, including his brother-in-law Osiander, Cranmer became the chief architect of England's new *Book of Common Prayer*, the first edition of which was published in 1549. Cranmer had two main aims – first, he wanted to see all worship conducted in the language of the people, so that they might understand what was said, and second, he wanted the liturgy to reflect what was now official teaching for a reformed Church. Anglicans often speak of a fundamental principle for worship – that the rules by which we pray are the rules of our belief, a principle first enunciated by Prosper of Aquitaine in the fifth century, but which was now applied with new vigour by Cranmer.

Many of the prayers published under Cranmer's leadership have become famous and well loved, and one of these is the Prayer of Humble Access. Cranmer appears to have written this prayer himself, but he drew on three Bible passages to formulate his words. The first is Matthew 8.8, where a centurion affirms his faith in Jesus' ability to heal his servant without even visiting his home, but merely by giving the command. The second is Mark 7.28, where the Syrophoenician woman challenges Jesus to heal her child. In that passage, Jesus initially declines, saying that the children of Israel were his chief concern, but the woman challenges Jesus by saying that even dogs could eat the crumbs that fell from the children's table. Third is the statement in Christ's teaching about Communion: 'Whoever feeds on my flesh and drinks my blood abides in me, and I in him' (John 6.56). Cranmer works these texts into one simple but direct prayer which has been used by Anglicans approaching Communion ever since, as it acknowledges both our faith and our fragility.

When we pray this prayer, let us hope it will teach us about an unassuming and modest way in which to approach God, seeking for the gifts of his mercy and grace in our lives:

We do not presume to come to this, your table, merciful Lord, trusting in our own righteousness, but in your manifold and great mercies.

We are not worthy to gather up the crumbs under your table, but you are the same Lord whose nature is always to have mercy.

Grant us, therefore, gracious Lord, so to eat the flesh of your dear Son, Jesus Christ, and to drink his blood, that we may evermore dwell in him, and he in us. Amen.

TWENTY-THREE

IGNATIUS LOYOLA
Not Counting the Cost

The same century that began with the Protestant Reformation also saw the renewal of the Catholic faith. Sometimes described by historians as the Counter-Reformation, since a great deal of its energy was directed towards re-establishing Catholicism in places where Protestantism had taken hold, it is better described as the Catholic Reformation, as it was a genuine renewal of Catholic devotion and vigorous evangelisation in its own right.

Spearheading the work of Catholic renewal was an Order of religious men named after Jesus himself – the Society of Jesus, or the Jesuits. It was founded in Paris in 1539 by a group of seven companions, led by Iñigo Lopez de Oñaz from Loyola, a fortress in northern Spain. Iñigo, or Ignatius, was from a noble family, and, like so many of the aristocratic class, was co-opted very early on into the military. Ignatius had joined the army at the age of seventeen, but at the Battle of Pamplona in 1521, his right leg was almost totally destroyed by a cannonball, and, despite careful surgery, Ignatius limped for the rest of his life.

His military career over, Ignatius had an extended period of recovery, during which he asked to be given books about his military heroes, but his sister-in-law only had books about Jesus and the lives of the saints to offer as reading matter. He was greatly influenced by the writings of Ludolph of Saxony, who encouraged people to enter into the biblical narrative by imagining themselves into the stories of the Gospels. It was the beginning of a religious conversion that upended his life. Experiencing desolation at the thwarting of a life as a noble knight, Ignatius found consolation in the service of the poor, and intense devotion to the Lord.

Meeting up with Peter Faber and Francis Xavier in Paris, Ignatius and four other companions pledged themselves to the service of Christ, and founded a Society that quickly became a major force in spreading the gospel throughout the world – 'Go, and set the world on fire' he is said to have commanded Francis Xavier who was setting off to preach the gospel in India.

Ignatius' Jesuits were at the forefront of many of the initiatives to defend Catholicism and to evangelise the world, but although their reputation was fearsome, their zeal was tempered by a deep commitment to the conversion of the whole of life to following Jesus. A number of contemporary portraits of Ignatius survive, from which the picture for this chapter is adapted.

Ignatius himself produced a spiritual manual, the *Spiritual Exercises*, which drew on the teachings of the Brethren of the Common Life, and the *Devotio Moderna* (Chapter 21), but which set out an intensely practical process by which a person could reflect on all aspects of their life and faith, and lay the ground for a change of heart and a renewed commitment to be a disciple of Jesus. Ignatius was also much influenced by the *Anima Christi* (Chapter 20), and made so much use of it in his writings that for many years he was believed to be its author. The *Spiritual Exercises* in their complete form constitute a retreat in silence and solitude under the guidance of a spiritual mentor, and is conducted over thirty days, in which consideration is given to God's mercy, the life of Jesus, the Passion of Jesus, and the Resurrection of Jesus and his gift of Love. Today, the *Spiritual Exercises* are as influential and popular as when Ignatius first taught them himself. They can be conducted in a number of forms, including adaptation to be undertaken alongside the ongoing commitments of daily life.

Indeed, this approach toward Christian discipleship, which brings heart and mind together in understanding the movement of God in a person's life, has been recognised as a distinct form of (Ignatian) spirituality and has found a new popularity in the twenty-first century among Christians of all denominations.

The popular Prayer of St Ignatius, of which he is the undoubted author, reflects a soldier's commitment to discipleship and perseverance, and urges us to a thorough-going journey of faith and service. It reminds me of the commitment of St Paul to service as an apostle, and his experience of perseverance (2 Corinthians 4.7–12).

> Teach us, good Lord, to be generous, and to serve you as you deserve; to give, and not to count the cost, to fight, and not to heed the wounds, to toil, and not to seek for any rest, to labour, and not to ask for any reward, except that of knowing that we are doing your will. Amen.

TWENTY-FOUR

TERESA OF AVILA
The Body of Christ

*Christ has no body but yours, no hands, no feet on earth
but yours. Yours are the eyes on which he looks out
compassionately on this world. Yours are the feet with which
he walks to do good. Yours are the hands with which he
blesses the world.*

Another of the great saints of the Catholic Reformation in the
sixteenth century was Teresa of Avila. Teresa became one of
the foremost mystics of her day, and her writings continue to
inspire with her bold visions and strong exhortations.

Born into a merchant family in 1515, Teresa always had a strong romantic streak, running away from home to fight the Moors when seven, and lapping up stories of knights errant, saints and heroes as a child. Her mother's death when she was eleven was a huge blow, however, and Teresa found herself more and more comforted by a devotion to the Virgin Mary. At twenty, she decided to enter the religious life, joining a local Carmelite convent, and giving herself to a life of contemplation and prayer. During this period, she gave herself over to practices aimed at subduing any physical urges towards indulgence, although her self-mortification did result in several periods of severe illness. As she recovered, she began to have intense mystical visions, and even experienced a form of religious ecstasy, in which she felt united with the presence of God. Like Catherine of Siena, these visions were often interpreted in a strongly physical way. One famous vision included Teresa experiencing her heart being pierced by a fiery lance thrust at her by an angel, which has inspired sensual and dramatic artistic representations.

I believe that we have to sit lightly to accounts of visionary experiences like this. They cannot be approached with the intellect, which tries to rationalise them and make sense of them – visions are essentially chaotic, and speak to us from a non-rational level. For Teresa, they appeared to leave her with an intense love of God, and a conviction of God's desire to redeem creation.

Teresa's own intense prayer and reflection grounded her with a spiritual wisdom that many sought to consult. She drew inspiration from *The Imitation of Christ* (Chapter 21), and wrote her own work, *The Way of Perfection*, which adapted many of the ideas that she had encountered. Her desire to see God's love in the world and to continue the mission of Jesus inspired some of her most famous words, which have been chosen to head this chapter. They remind us that it is for the Church, for us as disciples, to continue the work of healing and restoration which was begun by God in Jesus. The picture of Teresa is adapted from a portrait painted in Teresa's lifetime by Jan Narduck, an Italian native, who himself became a religious brother in Spain. It offers a far more down to earth image of Teresa than the eroticised sculptures of Bernini.

Teresa became a strong advocate of a harsher monastic routine, similar to that we have seen in David, Francis and Clare (Chapters 15–17). So often it seems that spiritual insight and physical austerity go hand in hand. Teresa undertook a reform of the Carmelite community, setting up her own stricter version in Avila, to the consternation of some. This example of reform found favour with the Church authorities, and Teresa found herself in demand to visit other monastic foundations, and to oversee the renewal of monastic life. It was not universally popular, and Teresa and her supporters found themselves subject to attacks and accusations from the Inquisition, to the extent that Teresa had to go into voluntary retirement. In 1579, Teresa was vindicated by the combined support of King Philip II and Pope Gregory XIII, and was permitted to establish her own order of the Discalced (barefoot) Carmelites.

When she died in 1582, her last words were: 'Time to move on. O my Lord and Spouse, the hour that I have longed for has come, it is time for us to meet one another.' Teresa was made a Doctor of the Church by Pope Paul VI in 1970, alongside Catherine of Siena, and her writings have always been cherished as profound sources of spiritual wisdom and exhortation.

I offer this prayer in which Teresa put all her life into God's hands to live out her faith, encapsulated in the passage that began this chapter:

Lord, grant that I may always allow myself to be guided by you, to follow your plans, and to accomplish what you will. Grant that, in all things great and small, today and all the days of my life, I may do what you ask of me. Help me to respond to the slightest prompting of your grace, so that I may be a trustworthy instrument of your honour. May your will be done, by me, in me and through me. Amen.

TWENTY-FIVE
THOMAS KEN
A Doxology

Sometimes our prayer can become very self-centred – a list of requests to God to act in our lives, or in the life of our community, friends or family, or in the world itself. Yet many of the psalms do not follow this model – instead they are a joyful acclamation of praise to a bountiful God. Worship should always go beyond our concerns, and focus upon the brightness of being on whom creation depends. It draws us into a bigger understanding of the universe, and reminds us that, in Christian belief, the universe is not vast and impersonal, but founded on love.

The prayer offered in this chapter is a doxology, that is to say, a short prayer ascribing praise to God the Holy Trinity. The doxology has taken several forms down through the Christian centuries, originally being added to the end of each psalm: Glory be to the Father, and to the Son, and to the Holy Spirit; as it was in the beginning, is now and shall be to the ages of ages. Amen.

This doxology in this chapter was written by the seventeenth-century Anglican bishop Thomas Ken, and was originally intended to close two hymns that Ken had written for the choir of Winchester College, a school for boys founded in 1382 by the Bishop of Winchester, William of Wykeham. The morning hymn is 'Awake, my soul, and with the sun' and the evening hymn 'Glory to thee, my God, this night'. The doxology has been a firm favourite in its own right ever since. Many people can sing it from memory, using a number of popular tunes. It can be sung to the well-known tune *Old 100th*, first published in the edition of the *Genevan Psalter* of 1551, when it can be sung as a round, or, with Alleluias added, to the German tune, 'Lasst uns erfreuen'. There is also a popular modern tune, composed by Jimmy Owens, which is widely used.

Thomas Ken was a pupil himself at Winchester College, which explains his affection for the school, but early reminiscences by friends recall his musical interest and talent. He was ordained in 1662, the year in which the monarchy was restored following the upheavals of the Civil War. He won royal favour, and was appointed as a Royal Chaplain, in the course of which he was expected to provide hospitality for King Charles II and his mistress, Nell Gwynne. The story is told that Ken, disapproving of the king's adultery, excused his inability to accommodate the king's mistress by saying that he had the builders in, and promptly ordered a team of builders to remove the roof from his lodging so that he could not be accused of being a liar.

The King, with characteristic good humour, remembered this, and appointed Ken as Bishop of Bath and Wells the following year. Ken fell out of favour with King James, as the bishop disapproved of that king's commitment to Roman Catholicism, and he was even committed to the Tower for refusing to agree emancipation laws for Catholics in England. We might have expected him, therefore, to welcome the Protestant William and Mary to the throne when they led the so-called 'Glorious Revolution' of 1688, but Ken's intense sense of integrity would not allow him to break his oath of allegiance to King James, and he had to retire from his see.

Ken is remembered as a kindly man, with huge integrity and grace, and his three hymns remain popular to this day. The picture I have included in this chapter is a version of a portrait of Bishop Ken painted by F. Scheffer shortly before Ken's death in 1711.

We can give thanks for the moderate example of holiness revealed in people like Bishop Ken, as well as some of the more dramatic heroes of the faith I have written about in this volume, for their heroic virtue can inspire, but quiet holiness also has its place. In using his doxology, we can bring to mind that we are called to praise God in all things, and recall the invitation of St Paul: 'Rejoice in the Lord always; again I will say, rejoice.' (Philippians 4.4):

Praise God from whom all blessings flow;
praise him all creatures here below,
praise him above, ye heavenly host;
Praise Father, Son and Holy Ghost.

TWENTY-SIX

JOHN NEWTON
How Sweet the Name of Jesus

The eighteenth century saw an explosion of hymn singing as part of Christian prayer life and worship. Hymns, songs of praise to God not within Holy Scripture like the Book of Psalms, had been incorporated into worship very early on in the life of the Church, although the Psalms had a much preferred status as part of Holy Writ. We've noted the work of Venantius Fortunatus and Rabanus Maurus in the early centuries of the Church (Chapters 10 and 13), but eighteenth-century hymn writers were different, in that they took metrical forms and popular tunes and utilised them in God's praise. In contrast to

Gregorian chant, metrical hymns became highly popular with lay people and carried worship out of the sphere of church ritual and into everyday life with the use of tunes that were highly memorable and hummable.

The story of one of the greatest hymn writers of all times is well known, but the life of John Newton is so remarkable that it bears retelling. John was born in London, and by the age of seven was taken off to make a living on the sea. In 1743, he was press-ganged into the Royal Navy against his will, and had an adventurous life, becoming part of the crew of a slaving ship, transporting slaves from West Africa to the Caribbean. At one point, he was abandoned in West Africa, and left effectively serving as a slave to a native African royal family, but in 1748, he was rescued by the captain of an English trading ship, the *Greyhound*, and brought back to England. On the voyage home, a great storm threatened the ship and, fearing for his life, Newton experienced a sudden conversion, as he prayed for God's mercy. Even so, it took some time for his views to be challenged by his Christian faith. He continued to work on slaving ships for a while, even as he came to the realisation that God had other plans for his life, and the implication that God's Kingdom was not compatible with slavery.

In 1764, Newton was finally ordained, and eventually came to minister to an evangelical congregation in London, where his preaching became famous and drew large crowds. Newton had huge influence on a number of other people, including Thomas Scott, who went on to found the Church Missionary Society, and William Wilberforce, who became a leading light in the movement to abolish slavery. Newton had himself realised the implications of his faith, and had become a great advocate of the abolition of slavery, speaking of his former trade as one 'which contradicts the feeling of common humanity, ... and a stain on our National character soon to be wiped out'. In 1788 he wrote: 'It will always be a subject of humiliating reflection to me that I was once an active instrument in a business at which my heart now shudders.'

Newton therefore stands as a witness to the life-changing power of faith, and his contribution to hymnody is a testimony to the power that Newton discovered in the gospel. From the 1760s onwards, Newton co-operated with the poet William Cowper in producing a large number of hymns, including hymns that have remained popular until this day such as 'Glorious Things of Thee are Spoken' and 'Amazing Grace'. The portrait in this chapter is adapted from portraits of Newton engraved during his lifetime. In 1900, a museum was opened to commemorate the partnership of John Newton and William Cowper, and the painter W. S. Wright drew on all the existing portraits of Newton to produce the oil painting on which my own portrait is based.

'How sweet the name of Jesus sounds' also ranks as one of Newton's most famous hymns; it demonstrates the nature of salvation and redemption, and the central place that the person of Jesus Christ must play in faith.

How sweet the name of Jesus sounds
in a believer's ear!
It soothes his sorrow, heals his wounds,
and drives away his fear.

It makes the wounded spirit whole
and calms the troubled breast;
'tis manna to the hungry soul,
and to the weary, rest.

Jesus, my Shepherd, Husband, Friend,
my Prophet, Priest, and King,
my Lord, my Life, my Way, my End,
accept the praise I bring.

Weak is the effort of my heart,
and cold my warmest thought;
but when I see Thee as Thou art,
I'll praise Thee as I ought,

Till then I would Thy love proclaim
with every fleeting breath;
and may the music of Thy name
refresh my soul in death.

TWENTY-SEVEN

JOHN WESLEY
The Covenant Prayer

Another pair of ministers who knew the power of hymnody were the brothers John and Charles Wesley. Between them, they wrote over 1,500 hymns, and this legacy proved to be the bedrock of a new tradition in the life of Christianity, Methodism. John was the fifteenth child of an Anglican cleric, and both he and his brother Charles, his parents' eighteenth child, studied in Oxford University. While at Oxford, John and Charles started an informal group of Christians, which met every morning between six and nine o'clock for prayer and Bible study. In their discipleship, they were heavily influenced by Thomas à Kempis and *The Imitation of Christ* (Chapter 21).

John and Charles sought to develop a 'method' by which their lives might be regulated, and growth into holiness promoted. This did not win them friends. They were ridiculed by others as the 'Holy Club' and as religious enthusiasts, and fanatics. This only spurred the Wesleys on, as they believed that persecution was a hallmark of genuine Christianity (Matthew 5.11). Their zeal may have been remarkable, but so was their attitude of love in the treatment of their neighbours. John Wesley was distinctive in his day for his merciful attitudes towards others, including those who were otherwise outcasts in society, such as homosexuals.

John and Charles felt deeply called to the mission field, and in 1735 set off to become missionaries in the Province of Georgia in the American colonies. Their experiences were not particularly successful, but their American mission brought John into contact with Moravian Christians, who impressed him with their simple faith and deep commitment to following Jesus. On returning to England, John and Charles were much influenced by the Moravian pastor Peter Boehler, who encouraged them both to 'preach faith until you have it'. It was among the Moravian worshippers in Aldersgate that John had his famous conversion, when his heart was 'strangely warmed', and his Christian faith confirmed. Although he and Charles were ordained Anglican clergy, John's 'enthusiasm' meant that he was shunned, and excluded from ministry in many Anglican churches. With the encouragement of George Whitefield, however, John did not hesitate to preach in the open air and in fields away from towns, attracting many with his message. With rejection by the established Church, but unwilling to see so much Christian energy and commitment go to waste, John incorporated his followers into a new society, the Methodists, which came into being after 1739.

Methodism, with its emphasis on repentance and conversion, quickly attracted large numbers of followers, and John was accorded a significant leadership role as Life President. The portrait I have included in this chapter is based upon a picture painted in 1766 by Nathaniel Hone. It shows Wesley at the age of sixty-two characteristically still conducting worship, and delivering sermons, in the open air, with a finger in his Bible marking the text on which he was preaching.

John Wesley believed that the commitment to following Christ needed frequent renewal, and in 1780, he published a book commending the use of an annual 'Covenant Service', in which congregations could unite to renew their faith and commitment. To this day, the Covenant Service is often used by Methodists at the start of a new year, and it speaks eloquently of what it means to be committed to Jesus Christ. It is directed towards a generous surrender to God's will and a readiness to serve him in the world.

As such, the Covenant Prayer has become much admired beyond Methodism, and is a useful resource for anyone who wishes to make a commitment as a Christian, or to express a renewed commitment to their faith. The prayer exists in a variety of forms, as you might expect for a prayer that has been so widely used. I would like to offer for use here a modern adaptation:

I am no longer my own, but yours.
Put me to what you will, place me with whom you will.
Put me to doing, put me to suffering.
Let me be put to work for you or set aside for you,
Praised for you or criticised for you.
Let me be full, let me be empty.
Let me have all things, let me have nothing.

I freely and fully surrender all things to your glory and service.
And now, O wonderful and holy God,
Creator, Redeemer, and Sustainer,
you are mine, and I am yours.
So be it.
And the covenant that I have made on earth,
Let it also be made in heaven. Amen.

TWENTY-EIGHT

CHRISTINA ROSSETTI
A Christmas Carol

We have seen how music and the power of words have contributed to and enriched Christian worship. Poetry too is a skill exercised by many in offering their praise to God and seeking to articulate the dynamics of faith.

One poet of the nineteenth century whose work has an enduring popularity is Christina Rossetti. Christina was born in London to a father who was an Italian refugee, and Frances Polidori, the friend of Mary Shelley and Lord Byron. Her brother, Dante Gabriel Rossetti, became an artist and went on to become the leader of the Pre-Raphaelite Brotherhood, which was a school of art introducing a fresh style of medievalism (going back before the artist Raphael) into modern art. Christina was educated at home, and like Ignatius and Teresa, was brought up on a diet of stories of the saints, of fairy tales and novels. She seems to have imbibed a lively Christian faith from her mother, and attended Anglican church services from an early age. She admired the work of poets like John Keats and Italian renaissance authors such as Dante and Petrarch. From 1842, Christina started publishing her own poetry. This poetry was widely praised at the time, and Rossetti has even been hailed by critics such as Basil de Sélincourt as 'all but our greatest woman poet', influencing Virginia Woolf, Gerard Manley Hopkins and Elizabeth Jennings. Life was not all high culture, however, and Christina also devoted herself to working in the St Mary Magdalene House of Charity in Highgate, which sought to help women who had been trafficked or caught up in prostitution.

I have included a portrait of Christina which is based upon one of a great many portraits by her brother, Dante Gabriel Rossetti. The model for my picture was painted in 1866. Christina complained that her brother's portraits all made her look the same, which might be regarded as a compliment, although Christina was not entirely enamoured of her brother's work, and felt that the Pre-Raphaelite Brotherhood stereotyped women, and turned them into figures of medieval fantasy.

Christina's Christian faith comes across in her poetry, and there are two poems that have been adapted as Christmas carols, 'In the Bleak Midwinter' and 'Love came down at Christmas'. 'In the Bleak Midwinter' was first published in 1872 in a poetry magazine, and then in Christina's first collection of poetry, *Goblin Market*, in 1875 under the title 'A Christmas Carol', so it is clear that Rossetti intended it from the first to be set to music and sung. It was made famous by being set to a popular tune by Gustav Holst in 1906, and adapted as a choir piece by Harold Darke in 1909. More recently, it has competed with others to be named as the world's most popular Christmas carol.

Carols were informal folk songs used by people outside of Church worship for popular devotion and entertainment in the medieval period, and they were originally composed in praise of Christian festivals throughout the year. Francis of Assisi (Chapter 16) not only popularised the use of a Christmas nativity scene, but he also encouraged the tradition of Christmas carols in the local language at a time when all worship in Church was conducted in Latin. In the medieval period it became tradition for carol singers to travel around the community singing songs and calling at people's homes in order to raise money for the poor or destitute, so today's carol singers are continuing an ancient tradition.

Such activities had often been connected to the midwinter tradition of Wassail when blessings were sought on the community's fruit trees, and ceremonies undertaken to seek for God's blessing on new life and the coming of Spring. However, it was only the nineteenth century that saw the publication of many collections of Christmas carols, and renewed their popular use. It was only from this time that carols began to be sung in church and seen as an acceptable contribution to the formal worship of the Church.

Christina's 'Christmas Carol' imagines the birth of Christ as taking place amidst snow and the sort of winter scene that is more appropriate to northern Europe than the Middle East, but it juxtaposes the humility and physicality of Jesus' birth with the theological reality of the Incarnation, inviting the reader to reflect on the gifts that were presented to the infant Jesus (although the shepherds' gifts are in fact pure invention), and on their own response of faith.

For us, such faith and reflection does not have to be confined to Christmas, even though most of us will look forward to singing this carol with relish in that context.

In the bleak mid-winter frosty wind made moan
Earth stood hard as iron, water like a stone;
Snow had fallen, snow on snow, snow on snow,
In the bleak mid-winter long ago.

Our God, heaven cannot hold Him nor earth sustain,
Heaven and earth shall flee away when He comes to reign:
In the bleak mid-winter a stable-place sufficed
The Lord God Almighty – Jesus Christ.

Enough for Him, whom cherubim worship night and day,
A breastful of milk and a mangerful of hay;
Enough for Him, whom Angels fall down before,
The ox and ass and camel which adore.

Angels and Archangels may have gathered there,
Cherubim and seraphim thronged the air;
But only His Mother in her maiden bliss
Worshipped the Beloved with a kiss.

What can I give Him, poor as I am?
If I were a Shepherd I would bring a lamb;
If I were a Wise Man I would do my part, –
Yet what I can I give Him, – Give my heart.

TWENTY-NINE

EDITH STEIN
The Journey

Edith Stein is one of the most intriguing religious figures of the twentieth century. She came from a Jewish background, and yet she converted to the Catholic faith. However, her Christian commitment manifested itself in a rigorous form, and Edith became a Discalced Carmelite nun (Chapter 24) and her Jewish Christian identity meant that she was ultimately martyred in the death camp of Auschwitz-Birkenau.

Although she was born into an observant Jewish family, Edith had become an agnostic by the time she was a teenager. She was an enthusiastic student, and achieved an excellent doctorate in Philosophy, with the highest accolade of being awarded her degree *summa cum laude*. On leaving university, however, she threw herself into the care of humanity, and took on work as a nursing assistant in an infectious diseases hospital.

It was on learning about the life of Teresa of Avila that Edith was drawn to Christianity, and she was baptised in 1922 into the Catholic Church. At first, she took up a teaching career, but with the rise of the Nazi party in Germany, she failed to meet the appropriate racial profiling to remain as a teacher, and Edith's developing and profound religious convictions persuaded her to enter the discalced Carmelite community in Cologne, where she took the religious name Teresa Benedicta of the Cross, in commemoration of her great love for Teresa of Avila, and for Benedict of Nursia, the founder of Benedictine monasticism. There are many pictures of Edith both before and after her profession as a Carmelite, but the picture I have chosen is an early portrait in her more carefree days, and itself based on family photographs.

With the advent of the Nazi movement in Germany, and their concern for racial purity, Edith was sent out of Germany by the order for her own safety to a convent in the Netherlands. It was not to have a happy ending, however, for with the Nazi occupation of the Low Countries, she was rounded up with other Catholics who had a Jewish background and sent to the concentration camps. In 1942 she was transferred to Auschwitz, and it is believed that in August that year she and her sister Rosa perished in the gas chambers.

Edith's philosophical studies have won the admiration of many thinkers, while her synthesis of Jewish and Christian beliefs, and her commitment to integrating the Christian revelation into her world view have made a profoundly distinctive contribution to the understanding of Christianity in the modern world.

However, it is her heroic virtue in the face of Nazi persecution that has also inspired much reverence. She was convinced of God's victory in Christ – 'Love is stronger than hatred', she wrote, 'and in the end there shall be only the fullness of love. If we accept the whole Christ in faithful self-giving, by choosing and walking in the way of the imitation of Christ, then he will lead us through his Passion and Cross to the glory of the Resurrection.' This faith sustained her as she faced great evil, from which she did not run away.

In the very early centuries of the Church, the Church Father Tertullian had written that 'The blood of the martyrs is the seed of the Church'. Throughout history the story of the crucified God, and Jesus' warning that following the path of righteousness would bring suffering, has enabled Christians under persecution to find strength and courage in the face of ostracism, torture and even death. Such fortitude has been met with wonder and awe by those who have witnessed it.

Yet the saints themselves have always been very modest about their achievements in holiness. For Edith, faith was a journey, in which only a little of the future was ever clear. She asked only for enough grace to complete the next stage of what was asked of her, confident that God would journey with her. Edith's prayer, which is offered at the close of this chapter, encapsulates such a philosophy, and draws on biblical imagery of the risen Jesus who walks besides his disciples on the path to Emmaus (Luke 24.13–35).

Perhaps we can pray it in the same spirit. We may never have to face the challenges that Edith faced in her life, or the reality of horrors such as were experienced in Auschwitz. However, we can share Edith's sense of agnosticism about the future, confident in the belief that God travels with us in the person of Christ. It is a faith to sustain and guide us whatever the world might throw at us.

O my God, fill my soul with holy joy,
and the courage and strength to serve you.
Kindle your love in me
and then walk with me along the next stretch
    of the road before me.
I do not see very far ahead,
but when I have arrived at the point where
    the horizon now closes down,
a new prospect will open before me and
    I shall meet it with peace.
Amen.

THIRTY

REINHOLD NIEBUHR
The Serenity Prayer

One twentieth-century prayer which has become widely acknowledged and used is 'the Serenity Prayer'. Its popularity is probably based on its accessibility – no doctrine of God is articulated, but the human values and attitudes that it invokes can find a universal reception. The prayer, in one of its extended forms, has been widely adopted and used by Alcoholics Anonymous, as part of their twelve step plan to assist people in their own process of recovery. It would be fair to say that, as it has become more and more popular, the prayer has also been widely mimicked, and even satirised.

We can be fairly certain that the prayer can be traced back to the twentieth-century American theologian and scholar Reinhold Niebuhr. Only fairly certain, because Niebuhr himself did not claim the credit for it until many years after it became widely known, and even then suggested that he may have inherited it from his reading of prayers from many ages.

The prayer was attributed to Niebuhr by his colleague and friend, Winnifred Wygal, although some say that it is Wygal herself who should be acknowledged as the author. The earliest reference to something like the Serenity Prayer comes in Wygal's diary in 1932, when she wrote that 'RN says that … the victorious man in the day of crisis is the man who has the serenity to accept what he cannot help and the courage to change what must be altered.' It was obviously the sort of statement to which Niebuhr himself referred as an example of his life philosophy – it fits with his writings and thought – but it was Wygal again who included the prayer in a book offering guidance on the construction of liturgy and worship for use by women in business in 1940, and perhaps Wygal is due more credit than is usually given to her. Here is the prayer as it was published by her:

O God, give me the serenity to accept what cannot be changed, the courage to change what can be changed, and the wisdom to know the one from the other.

From this point on, the prayer became widely adopted and disseminated. The American Federal Council of Churches included it in a prayer book for army chaplains in the Second World War, and it was picked up by Alcoholics Anonymous in America in the 1940s, originally as 'The AA Prayer'. It was also adopted by the greeting cards company Hallmark in their publications and gifts, and so became widely disseminated. Niebuhr himself accepted credit for its authorship at this stage, and was known to quote it in his sermons, although later versions of the prayer became more and more elaborate.

Reinhold Niebuhr was one of the most influential American Protestant thinkers of the twentieth century. He was the child of German immigrants to America, and was born in 1892. He was ordained in the Evangelical tradition in 1915, in a Church pastoring German-speaking communities in the States, where he became noted for fighting against racial discrimination, and for his sympathies with the working classes. He became more widely known as a religious thinker in America in the period after the Second World War, and wrote about the interaction between religion and politics in books such as *The Children of Light and the Children of Darkness*. A quote that is typical of his thinking, and demonstrates his interest in the social implications of the gospel, is 'Man's capacity for justice makes democracy possible, but his inclination to injustice makes democracy necessary.'

The challenges of the Second World War made a deep impact upon him, and he became more pessimisitic about human nature, instead placing more emphasis on the biblical requirement for conversion and faith. He nevertheless maintained a broad view of Christian theology, taking issue with conservatives about what he believed was their naïve view of the scriptures, and with liberals because of their optimistic view of human nature.

Niebuhr's ideas have influenced thinkers and fighters for social justice such as Martin Luther King, and Barack Obama cited him as his favourite philosopher and theologian. His academic career was remarkably straightforward. In 1928, Niebuhr was appointed a professor at the Union Theological Seminary in New York, and he remained there, in the same post, until his retirement in 1960. The picture for this chapter is based upon a photograph taken in his study towards the end of his life in 1966.

Despite its popularisation, the Serenity Prayer still has wisdom to offer. It balances the call to vigorous action and engagement with the world, with a readiness to offer a practical focus on what is achievable. It calls upon God to provide what is lacking in human wisdom, even if it does not explicitly acknowledge him as the source of such gifts. It is a prayer that we can profitably use in all sorts of situations and in life.

God, give me grace to accept with serenity
the things that cannot be changed,
Courage to change the things
which should be changed,
and the Wisdom to distinguish
the one from the other. Amen.

THIRTY-ONE
LEONELLA SGORBATI
One Day

The dislocation of the two World Wars brought an end to the imperial age of Europe, and ushered in a new awareness of the fragility of human existence, and its vulnerability to corruption. Christians had been persecuted under the totalitarian governments that had come to power, especially where they had stood up to authority. However, the end of the twentieth century and the beginning of the twenty-first have seen a new context in which martyrdom is closer to the kind experienced by the early Christian communities as the perception of Christianity has changed, so that it is seen as the superstition of a former age, or identified as an alien intrusion into other cultures, and a leftover, perhaps, of the imperial age.

The twenty-first century has witnessed a growing number of martyrs in different contexts, and the bravery that they have shown has borne witness to Christian faith in a way that still earns respect and veneration. In 2015, for example, twenty-one Coptic Christians were killed on a beach in Libya by Islamist revolutionaries. In this case, it has been the witness of their families, who grieved their cruel and public murder but nevertheless found consolation in the love of God and offered forgiveness to their killers, which has become a striking example of a faith in God, even in the face of testing such as most of us would wish to avoid.

In this, they join Christians from the first century who have never been afraid of martyrdom. The Book of Acts records the death of the first martyr, Stephen, and speaks about how he was able to forgive his killers even as they stoned him. (Acts 7.54–60). Whether it be Polycarp in the first century (Chapter 4), or the very real witness of young women like Perpetua and Felicity in the third century, death for the cause of Christ became almost something to be embraced. There are other names, such as Francis Xavier, who have been touched upon in this book, who down through the centuries, have joined witnesses like Edith Stein, in paying the ultimate price for their faith.

The writer of the Epistle to the Hebrews in the New Testament spoke of the Christian Church as being surrounded by a cloud of witnesses (Hebrews 12.1), and that great company of saints and martyrs are being added to even in our own day.

One such is Leonella Sgorbati, who was martyred in Somalia in 2006. Leonella was born in Gazzola in Italy in 1940. By the age of sixteen she had decided that her vocation in life was to become a religious sister, and in 1963 she joined the

Consolata Missionary Sisters, a twentieth-century order who describe their mission as to bring the consolation of Jesus Christ to the people they serve, and to enhance the integrity of creation. Leonella trained as a nurse in England as part of the order before being sent out to Kenya, where she became a midwife and, subsequently, a senior tutor at the order's School of Nursing in Meru, Kenya. In 2002, she moved to Somalia, in order to set up a new nursing school in Mogadishu, even though the government of Somalia was becoming increasingly strident in supporting Islam and discouraging a Christian presence. Leonella was aware of the rising possibility that she would encounter violence. Early in 2006, she is recorded as saying: 'I know that there is a bullet with my name on it. I don't know when it will arrive, but as long as it does not arrive, I will stay in Somalia ... I cannot be afraid and at the same time love. I choose to love.' Remarkably, she said: 'I pray that one day, the Lord will take my life, as a sacrifice of love, this is my desire.'

This readiness to face death, even to seek it out, can be bewildering, since it flies in the face of any common sense. However, in the context of service and a deep belief that God has called them to a particular service and mission, Christians often find the conviction that their work and witness is more important than life itself, and that to abandon it would be to abandon God's will for their lives. It is not so much that we should seek death, but that we should be unafraid if death becomes a risk in the circumstances when the ministry to which God calls us comes under threat. It was the same refusal to bow to the demand that we should abandon faith and calling from the enemies of faith that led to the quiet but determined witness of Edith Stein (Chapter 29).

On 17 September 2006, Leonella was shot in the back three or four times by two gunmen who emerged from a taxi near her children's hospital in Mogadishu as she was in the street taking her lunch break. She was killed together with her driver and bodyguard. As people rushed to help her, her final words were 'I forgive, I forgive, I forgive.'

The cross that she wore has been deposited in the Basilica of St Bartholomew in Rome, which houses a growing collection of relics of modern martyrs from all denominations, including the prayer book of Oscar Romero, and mementos of the Anglican martyrs of Papua New Guinea. Together they make a compelling and moving tribute to the reality of present-day martyrdom, and a reminder that in many parts of the world, martyrdom remains a real and present possibility.

Most of the people who read this book will never be called to face the possible martyrdom that was faced by Leonella. We can only speculate about whether we would have the courage to continue in ministry when challenged, especially if there is a real danger to life. We have to trust that God will not bring us to that point of testing, or that if he does, he will supply us with the strength we need.

For most of us, however, life can be offered in the service of God's love in much more humble, even humdrum, ways. We can nevertheless aspire to live with the same dedication exhibited by Leonella, and those others whose example of life and prayer call us to our own commitment, and to say with her:

Lord, accept my life as a sacrifice of love.
This is my desire.